PORTRAIT OF ELIZABETH SAGER HELM AT 88 YEARS OF AGE

LORINDA BEWLEY
and The
WHITMAN MASSACRE

By

MYRA SAGER HELM

Pacific Northwest National Parks & Forests Association
83 S. KING STREET SUITE 212 SEATTLE, WASHINGTON 98104 (206) 442-7958

Printed in the United States of America by the Pacific Northwest National Parks and Forests Association, a non-profit corporation managed by a Board of Directors. Its purpose is to provide for the enhanced enjoyment and understanding of visitors to its areas of operation in the states of Washington, Oregon, and Idaho.

To

My Mother

Elizabeth Sager Helm

THE AUTHOR

Myra Sager Helm is a daughter of Elizabeth Sager Helm, one of the adopted children of Dr. Marcus Whitman.

I wish to say that this is a truthful story of my grandmother, Esther Lorinda Bewley Chapman and her experiences at the Whitman Massacre.

MRS. MARY G. MILLER

Mary Miller
3347 S. E. Belmont St.,
Portland, Oregon

INTRODUCTION

It was about 50 *years ago, that I interviewed Elizabeth Sager Helm. In fact, I knew and interviewed three members of the Sager family, who were at the Whitman Mission, when Dr. Whitman, his wife, and others at the Mission were killed by the Cayuse Indians. Matilda Jane Sager Delaney, issued a book on her experiences at the Mission during the hard years that followed the massacre. I have known Myra Sager Helm for many, many years. She has a host of friends, and is writing this book to perpetuate the memory of her mother, and other members of the Sager family, as well as Dr. and Mrs. Whitman.*

Myra Sager Helm is a painter of unusual ability. During the past 40 *years, she has supported herself by her brush, painting Mt. Hood and other scenic beauty spots of the Oregon Country. She has undoubtedly told you, or will tell you, details which will be of interest not only to the reviewers of her book but to those who read the book. She is of the stuff of which the Oregon pioneers were made; dependable, a person in whom you can place your trust, and a person who makes and keeps friends. I think I have said all that is necessary to tell you of her character and accomplishments. I hope the reviewers will treat her kindly, and I know you will do all you can to promote the sales of her book and to make it a success.*

FRED LOCKLEY

TABLE OF CONTENTS

Part One

Part Two

Part Three

Appendices

PART ONE

LORINDA BEWLEY
AND
THE WHITMAN MASSACRE

Late in September, 1847, a long emigrant train was slowly toiling up the divide above Powder River Plain, near what is now Baker, Oregon.

The roads were deep with dust and full of chuck holes. In many places it had been worn to bedrock by the hundreds of wagons that had passed over the Old Oregon Trail. The wagons lurched from side to side, the weary oxen straining at their yokes. Parts of wagons and dead oxen were strewn along the way. Now and then an ox would drop from exhaustion from the long and toilsome trip from the shores of the Missouri.

Women and children were walking to lighten the load, as the failing strength of the cattle was a constant worry. Grass was scarce and they had not time to lay-by to let them graze. It was getting late and they feared a snowstorm when crossing the Blue Mountains.

The weary emigrants pushed steadily on, hoping soon to reach the valley of the Grande Ronde. These brave and hardy pioneers, never complaining, were nearing the promised land — where a man and wife could take 640 acres of fertile land. A land free from black slavery, and chills and fever. A land of freedom, with hospitality and brotherly love among all early settlers, and which is still found in the hearts of their descendents.

Captain Bewley, leader of the emigrant train who was riding in advance, signaled the weary train to halt.

"Better rest a spell," he said, "the cattle are pretty well worn out."

He dismounted to rest his horse and gazed across the plain at the distant range of mountains, blue and mysterious in the approaching evening. Suddenly there shot up into the still evening sky a stately column of smoke. At once, all eyes caught it, and as they watched, immediately and farther to the north, another column arose.

The scouts in advance wheeled and came swiftly back. "Injun signals!" they shouted. "What do you make of that, Captain?"

"Sure looks bad," the Captain replied. "We can't turn back — have to keep going. Pass the word along for the wagons to keep close together and see that your guns are loaded. We want to be ready for a surprise!"

"The Injuns out here are not on the warpath, are they Captain?" a man asked.

"Not the Cayuse or the Nez Perces," the Captain replied, "But we were warned to look out for the Snake Injuns. I hear them fellers are a bad lot — always on the warpath, and we're getting into their country now. Could be their signal smokes."

The men looked at their wives and children. The women gathered their little ones close, whispering anxiously among themselves, hushing the voices of the frightened children.

That night extra guards were stationed and every precaution taken to prevent a surprise attack, but the night passed quietly.

They made an early start next morning and saw no further signs of Indians, and on the third day reached the rim of the Grande Ronde Valley. The long train halted and the emigrants hurried forward, gathering around the Captain.

They gazed with surprise and delight at this most beautiful

little valley in Oregon. Almost circular in shape, surrounded by lofty mountains, covered with pine, spruce and hemlock, level as far as the eye could see, and covered with luxuriant Bunchgrass or Wild Clover.

The Grande Ronde River and several smaller streams, looked like silver threads as they wound through the valley, their banks lined with poplar and alder trees that furnished abundant shade for the campers.

Smoke curled up from many Indian camps dotted over the valley, and hundreds of spotted horses grazed nearby. This little valley was beloved by the Indians for many generations. They called it, "The Valley Of Peace."

It is said that if an enemy Indian came into the valley he was treated as a friend as long as he remained. This was a favorite meeting place for the tribes of that region. Here they held their councils, traded with each other, and raced their horses and gambled — a favorite sport with them.

It was also a favorite hunting ground. The mountains were full of game of all kinds. The women tanned the deer skins for clothing and many other uses.

The Camas grew here in abundance, and now was the time for gathering it. It was the principal winter food of these tribes, and to prepare it was the exclusive work of the Indian woman. The Camas is a root, or bulb, looking much like an onion in shape and color, and was greatly prized by the Indians. To prepare it, they dug a round hole in the ground, filled it half full of hot stones which was then covered with grass, then filled nearly full of Camas, and then covered with grass and dirt. When it is taken out it is black in color and has a sweet taste much like that of figs.

As the emigrants gazed into the valley they saw riding towards them a small band of Indians.

The Scouts shouted, "Here they come, Captain!"

One of the Indians detached himself from the band and with hand raised in friendly salute, rode swiftly towards the waiting emigrants. Pulling his horse to an abrupt halt he said, "I am Five Crows, Chief of the Cayuse, Dr. Whitman's Indians. He has sent us out to meet you with a pack train of fresh vegetables, flour and medicine. He heard there are sick among you."

"Yes, many sick. Couldn't go much farther without help," the Captain said.

"Dr. Whitman sends us out to meet every train," said the Chief.

Captain Bewley looked in amazement at this Indian. The finest looking he had ever seen. Of medium height, well built, regular features, dressed like a white man of that time in a buckskin suit, beautifully beaded, with his hair cut short and wearing a wide brimmed hat.

The tense moment passed and seeing that the Indians were friendly, the men came running forward, crowding around the Chief shaking his hand.

Five Crows and his men who had now arrived were mounted on splendid spotted horses, a breed entirely new to the emigrants.

"Chief," said one of the men, "where did you get those spotted horses? I never saw anything like them. I thought we had fine horses in Kentucky, but nothing like these!"

"A long time ago," said Five Crows, "our Fathers brought them from far over the mountains. We think Spanish. They are very strong and stand long rides and are trained to swim the rivers. Some are very swift race horses. Chief Teloukaike gave Dr. Whitman one of his best and he rides many miles to see the sick."

"The Indians out here do not seem to resent the white people coming among them," said Captain Bewley.

"No," said Five Crows, "Dr. Whitman does not allow them to settle in our country. They all go down to the Valley of the Willamette."

"Chief," said Captain Bewley, "three days ago we saw two smoke signals. What did that mean?"

"It was the Cayuses signaling the Nez Perces, far to the North, that an emigrant train was coming, and for them to meet us with flour from Mr. Spaulding's mill. Other emigrants had eaten all of Dr. Whitman's flour and he had to send a long way to get this."

"Early sun I leave to hunt the deer. To be gone a week or two. My men are camped in the valley. You camp with us tonight and we will protect you from the Snake Indians."

"That suits us," said the Captain, "and with fresh vegetables and flour again we'll forget all the hardships of the trail."

"Do you hear that, wife? We will have flour and potatoes for supper tonight!"

Telling the men to lock the wheels of their wagons with chains before starting down the steep and rocky mountain to the valley below, the Chief wheeled his horse and rode back along the train of the wagons, lifting the wagon cover of each, looking for a white girl with golden hair and blue eyes, like Narcissa Whitman."

This had been his custom ever since the first wagon train. He could not understand why he could not have a white wife when many white men were married to Indian girls.

(Dr. Whitman once said, "Five Crows wanted to be like a white man more than any other Indian I've ever known.")

At the wagon of Captain Bewley he found pretty Lorinda, the Captain's daughter, very ill with that plague of Missouri, chills and fever. The stopping of the wagons had lulled

Lorinda into a sound sleep so she didn't see the Chief looking at her. Five Crow's heart gave a leap. Here, at last, was the girl of his dreams! Lorinda was golden-haired and blue-eyed, but whose was she?

Turning to the driver of the team, Crocket Bewley, he said, "Your woman?"

"My sister," replied Crocket.

"She pretty," said the Chief. "Hair like sunshine; she sick?"

"Yes," said Crocket, "very sick. Chills and fever, and tired out from the long trip."

"You hurry to Dr. Whitman, he make her well," said Five Crows, and wheeled his horse, rode to the head of the train and led them down into the valley.

Soon the weary oxen were unyoked and turned out to feast on the luxurious bunchgrass. Supper fires were glowing and preparations were under way for a feast.

Crocket moved over to his mother's fire. "Mother," he begged, "can't we have some hot biscuits tonight? Seems like an awful long time since we had any."

"Of course we can, son," she replied. "Rake up the coals and get the Dutch oven hot and I'll soon have the biscuits ready to bake."

Crockett's eyes danced as he hurried to obey. He loved hot biscuits, and his mother was an expert in the art of baking them in that Dutch oven.

The Captain came strolling over. "About time to bring Lorinda out, mother?" he asked.

"Yes, bring her out to get some fresh air. Maybe she can eat something tonight, we've got so many good things," said Mrs. Bewley.

Carefully the Captain and Crockett lifted the sick girl from the wagon and handed her down. Five Crows, standing near, quickly drew his own handsome Hudson's Bay blanket from his shoulder and with all the grace of a Cavalier, spread it upon the ground and the sick girl was laid tenderly upon it.

Five Crows hurried away but returned soon with a choice piece of venison which he presented to Mrs. Bewley, saying, "For the sick girl. My men bring you all the flour and potatoes you want."

Lorinda looked at the venison as her mother cooked it over the open fire and said, "Oh, Mother, that does look so good. I believe I can eat some of it."

Mrs. Bewley turned to the Chief. "Thank you, Five Crows," she said. "The good Lord sent you. I don't know what we would have had to eat tonight." Five Crows smiled and turning, went back to his camp.

"That's a mighty fine man, Mother," said the Captain as they sat about their supper, "and handsome too, even if he is an Indian. I'd like to know more about him."

The emigrants sat down that night to a veritable feast and arose from it refreshed, and with renewed strength and courage. Gone was the fear of the Indians and a feeling of security prevailed. Laughter was heard for the first time in many weeks, and here and there a woman burst into a snatch of a song as she washed the dishes.

"Let's have a dance folks, what do you say?" cried a young fellow.

"Yes, lets!" chorused a dozen voices at once, "bring out your shovels boys and lets clear a place!"

There was a scurrying to get the tools and the ground was leveled and on the evening air came the merry sound of "tuning up" the fiddles and banjos. The swains scurried through the camp selecting their partners, and soon the "sets" were formed for the quadrille.

Old Jim Connor, the official caller, tall, lean, pants tucked in his boots, jumped upon a wagon tongue. Shifting his quid of tobacco over in his other cheek, he called out, "All set?" Then, swaying to the music, he sang out, "All join hands and circle to the left, swing that gal beside you. Sashay round and come right back, to the gal you left behind you. Aloman left and do-se-do, and go half way to greet 'em —right and left, and balance all, and squeeze 'em when you meet 'em."

Old Jim, getting well warmed up, jumped off the wagon tongue, and bowing his legs and cutting pigeon-wings, hopped about among the dancers calling his changes and creating howls of laughter. The curious Indians gathered around, looking on in amazement. They had never seen anything like this before.

Captain and Mrs. Bewley stood watching the dancers, relieved and happy to see them enjoying themselves. Five Crows came over to them.

"My men do not understand the white man's war dance," he said gravely.

"This is not a war dance, Chief," said the Captain. "The white people do not dance a war dance. It has always been the custom of the white people to dance for amusement. The young people are very happy tonight, and we have you to thank for it."

"It makes me happy to see them so," said the Chief.

Mrs. Bewley looked thoughtful. "Chief," she said, "are you a Christian Indian?"

"I am a member of Mr. Spalding's church," he replied. "I see the great good it does my people and I encourage it."

"You speak English well," said the Captain, "where were you educated?"

"I spent my Winters at Mr. Spalding's school," he replied. "My people are very anxious to learn the white man's ways. Many Indians now have their little farms and raise their own vegetables, so they do not have to travel so far to trade with other Indians or go on long buffalo hunts. Mr. and Mrs. Spalding are like father and mother to us. The Indians all love Mrs. Spalding. She is a very brave woman."

After watching the dancers for a short time longer the Chief strode away to his own camp.

Soon the merrymakers tired and the camp settled down for the night, tired but happy. Here, for the first time in many weeks, they felt safe and went to sleep without guards. The next morning they traded their worn-out cattle for fresh horses, and made good time towards the Whitman Mission.

Dr. Whitman and Mr. Spalding taught their Indians to break their horses during the Winter, and trade them to the emigrants for their worn-out cattle, and the Indians were growing rich and many had large herds.

The Bewley family, feeling the immediate need of securing medical attention for Lorinda hastened ahead of the train and in the early evening sighted the Mission.

Framed in the sunset glow, it looked to them like a Paradise. The main Mission house was a large adobe, story and a half, built in the form of a "T," painted white, and, to their surprise, had a garden of old-fashioned flowers, hollyhock and marigolds, all carefully tended. There were curtains at the windows giving the impression of a comfortable and prosperous home. Besides the Mission house there was a large house built for the emigrant families that stayed there every Winter, and a Grist Mill and Blacksmith Shop.

In the fall of 1836 Dr. Marcus Whitman and his bride Narcissa, accompanied by Henry Spalding and his young wife, Eliza, came across the plains and mountain ranges to the then unknown Oregon country as missionaries among the Indians.

Mr. Spalding settled among the Nez Perces at Lapwa, and Dr. Whitman among the Cayuses twenty-five miles from Fort Walla Walla, a Hudson's Bay post on the Columbia River.

Teloukaike, the War Chief, claimed the land in this locality and gave Dr. Whitman his choice of location, and he selected a sort of peninsula formed by the Walla Walla River. The Indians called this Waiilatpu, meaning "The Place of Rye Grass," and this was a favorite resort of the Cayuses and Walla Walla Indians who camped here when not away on their hunting trips.

The Cayuse Indians were proud and haughty, the richest Indians in that part of the country, owning large bands of their wonderful spotted ponies. After the emigrants began coming to Oregon they acquired large herds of cattle.

The Cayuse tribe was closely associated, and intermarried with the Nez Perces, a larger, but less warlike, tribe. The Cayuse tribe had their own system of government, the tribe being divided into three camps, each governed by a head chief and several sub-chiefs. Each head chief governed his people as he pleased without interference from the other head chiefs.

There was the camp of Teloukaike at Waiilatpu, where Dr. Whitman had his Mission, about twenty-five miles from Fort Walla Walla, and extending to the Umatilla River. The camp of Camaspole lay between Fort Walla Walla and Waiilatpu, and the camp of Five Crows and his half-brother Young Chief, east of the Umatilla River.

In the fall of 1844 the emigrants brought to the Mission

the forlorn little Sager children, whose father and mother had died on the plains, leaving seven children, John fourteen, Frank twelve, Catherine ten, Elizabeth eight, Matilda six, Louise three, and the baby, Henrietta, five months old. Dr. and Mrs. Whitman took them to their hearts and treated them as their own.

The Whitman's only child, little golden-haired Alice Clarissa, was born a few months after the arrival of Dr. Whitman and his wife at Waiilatpu and lived to gladden their hearts only two and a half years, when she was drowned in the Walla Walla River. Little Alice Clarissa was a beautiful child and could speak and sing in the Indian language better than in English. The Indians almost worshipped her.

The next day after she was born the house was crowded with Indians curious to see her. Everything about her was strange to them, the color of her skin, her eyes and hair, and they could not understand why she did not break in two when not strapped to a board. The old Chief Teloukaike said, "She is little white Cayuse because she was born on Cayuse land." After her death the Indians did not come around the Mission for some time as they were very superstitious.

In later years Mrs. Whitman wrote to her parents, "God has taken away our own dear child so that we could open our hearts to all the little orphan children." Alice Clarissa was buried on a hill where Mrs. Whitman could step to the door and see her grave.

The summer of 1847 passed quietly and happily at the Mission, the children sleeping out of doors as had been their custom every Summer, riding horses, bathing in the river, and roaming over the hills picking flowers for Mrs. Whitman's collection of pressed wild flowers.

In the Fall of 1847 Dr. Whitman and John Sager took two wagons down to The Dalles to bring back supplies that had been shipped to him. Coming back he discovered a much better route, farther back from the river, thus missing several hills.

There was a large emigration that year. Soon after his return from The Dalles, Dr. Whitman got on his horse and piloted the emigrants over this new route. The welfare of the settlers of Oregon was always foremost in his heart, and he did everything in his power to assist them. He had just returned when little Matilda Sager, playing in the mission yard with the other children, looked up and saw the emigrants coming. Running excitedly into the house, she shouted, "Father! There's an emigrant wagon coming!"

Dr. Whitman hurried outside, saying to Mrs. Whitman, "That must be the wagon train we have been expecting; the one with so much sickness among them."

Captain Bewley, riding up in front of the house, met Dr. Whitman hastening to meet him.

Dr. Whitman was a man of medium height, broad shoulders showing great strength and endurance. Quick of step, deep set dark blue eyes, dark hair tinged with gray, rugged features, smooth shaven except for a short beard under his chin, looking very much like early pictures of Abraham Lincoln of whom he was a distant relative. He came of a long line of illustrious ancestors, was a man of great determination. A man of better education than most of those in Oregon at that time.

The Sager children adored him; he never corrected them. Sometimes he would turn his back and laugh heartily at their mischief. He left all the disciplining to Mrs. Whitman. She had a natural gift of managering children while she was strict with them, she was always kind and just. Mother loved her dearly.

"My name is Bewley, sir," he introduced himself. "Captain of the wagon train camped below here. I have brought my daughter who is very bad off with chills and fever, to see what you can do for her. The Indians say you are a great medicine man. There is a violent form of measles in the train, and many have died on the trail. They will lay over awhile and rest. They are in need of medical attention. Many of the wagons will be late getting in tonight. I'm afraid they will have difficulty in finding their way."

"Oh no," said Dr. Whitman, "my Indians always know when a wagon is late and they will build bonfires on the hills to guide them in."

"Get down, man! Get down and come in!" cried Dr. Whitman, shaking him heartily by the hand. "After supper I'll go right down and see them."

"Your Indians seem very friendly toward the white people passing through their country; I am surprised," said Captain Bewley.

"Yes, the Indians have a great desire to own cattle, and they are becoming rich off the worn-out stock they are trading for," said Dr. Whitman. "They plan all year for meeting the trains in the Fall, and some go as far as Fort Hall to pick up the worn-out cattle. They are beginning to learn the value of money, and I'm told they are getting to be sharp traders."

"The Indians were never more quiet than now," he continued. "There have been some deaths among them — of important Indians. But as far as the Indians are concerned, our prospects of permanently remaining among them was never more favorable than at the present time."

"I hear that you have a large family of orphan children that you have adopted as your own," said Captain Bewley.

"Yes, we have," replied the Doctor. "My wife often feels distressed to think she has so little time to do personal work among the Indians when there is so much to be done, but she consoles herself with the thought of the good the Indians receive by seeing so many white children growing up in their midst."

"Perrin, my nephew, and the oldest," continued the Doctor, "is able to read and speak their language well, and when I am gone from home he takes my place and holds meetings with them, and this delights them very much."

Just then Mrs. Whitman, a tall, beautiful, golden-haired woman, came to the door and hastened down to greet them.

Waving his hand toward the wagon, Captain Bewley said, "This is my wife, my son Crocket, and my daughter, Lorinda."

The family was cordially received into the hospitable home of Dr. Whitman and in a few days Lorinda was very much improved.

The next week the Bewleys began planning to continue their journey on to the Willamette Valley, and Mrs. Whitman, having become very much attached to Lorinda (being much pleased by her refinement and manners) begged her to remain at the Mission during the Winter to help with the children and continue her studies.

"We have hired a good teacher for the Winter," said Mrs. Whitman.

"But, Mrs. Whitman," objected Mrs. Bewley, "how will she get down to us in the Spring?"

"If you will let her stay," promised Mrs. Whitman, "I will see that she gets safely to you.

"Anyway," said Dr. Whitman, "I haven't got her chills and fever broken yet, and it isn't safe for her to go on."

"I would like to stay if Crocket could stay too," said Lorinda.

"That will be all right," said Dr. Whitman, "I can give him some work."

"Well, Mother," said Captain Bewley, "I guess that is the best plan. We can go down to the Valley and get located, and send for the youngsters in the Spring. We'd better plan to leave about the day after tomorrow."

"Oh, Mother," cried Lorinda, "I hate to stay behind, but Mrs. Whitman needs me, and I love her so much already that maybe I won't be so lonesome after all. Then too, I must finish my studies if I am to teach school next Spring."

And so it was arranged.

The night of Bewley's arrival, Dr. Whitman visited the emigrant camp and found many sick. Upon his return he said to his wife, "That's the worst case of measles I've ever seen, and I'm afraid it will spread among the Indians. If it does, it will prove fatal to those that still hold to the old custom of sweat baths."

"Let us trust to Divine Providence that it will not spread," said Mrs. Whitman.

But before a month passed, it had spread, and several of the most influential Chiefs had died. The Doctor's entire family was also stricken, as well as the families of several that were wintering at the Mission. Dr. Whitman was kept going day and night.

One afternoon Five Crows rode over from his Lodge on the Umatilla and talked long and earnestly with Dr. Whitman. When the Doctor returned to the house, Mrs. Whitman asked, "What does Five Crows want?"

The Doctor smiled, "He has fallen deeply in love with Lorinda and wants to marry her," he said. "He offers a hundred horses, the pick of his herd, rich furs and Hudson Bay blankets."

"What did you tell him, Marcus?" inquired Mrs. Whitman.

"I told him white men did not sell their daughters. The

daughters made their own choice, and then the fathers gave them to the men to be their helpmates. But he wasn't satisfied, and asked me to plead for him. I felt sorry for him. He just didn't seem to know how to go about courting in a white man's ways."

Mrs. Whitman laughed.

"But a white girl could do a lot worse than to marry Five Crows, Narcissa," he continued. "He is well educated, and the wealthiest Indian in the whole country."

"But you wouldn't have Lorinda marry him, would you, Marcus?" exclaimed his wife.

"No, of course not," he laughed, "but I'll have a good joke on Lorinda."

About this time the Catholic priests had arrived at Fort Walla Walla, coming from England on a Hudson's Bay boat.

Dr. Whitman's friend, Mr. McKinley, at Fort Walla Walla, had been retired, and the Catholic half-breed McBain had taken his place. McBain did everything he could to help the priests get in touch with the Indians who were in favor of the priests as missionaries. He had several meetings with the Indians of Dr. Whitman's Mission, with the sulking Teloukaike, and his two sons, Edward and Clark, and Tamayhas and Tamsucky.

Clark and Edward, the two sons of Teloukaike, the war chief of the Cayuses, were in favor of having the priests as missionaries, and tried to get their father to give them land in sight of Dr. Whitman's Mission.

Young Chief, a half-brother of Five Crows, was a Catholic, and he gave the priests a log cabin on the Umatilla River, about forty-five miles from the Whitman Mission, and a quarter mile from the lodge of Five Crows. The priest moved to this place on the 26th of November, 1847. About this time, Rev. Spalding arrived at the Mission with his little daughter, Eliza, 10 years old, who was to attend school that Winter with Dr. Whitman's children.

Rev. Spalding and Dr. Whitman planned to attend a Council held by the Indians and priests, and persuade the priests, if possible, to allow the Indians to have the say as to whether Catholic or Protestant missionaries should remain among them. The feelings of the Indians were that both missionaries could not occupy the same field. The principal chief Ellis, said, "It will do for the French and English to have two religions, as they have laws; but for Indians, who have no laws, it will not do. We have one religion, with which we are satisfied. If the Catholics come into the country there will be fighting immediately."

Should the Indians prefer the Catholic Missionaries, Rev. Spalding and Dr. Whitman were ready to give up their Missions and retire to the Willamette Valley — but the blow struck too soon!

That evening, an Indian runner came from the Umatilla with word for the Doctor to come at once to attend the sick, among them being the wife of Tamayhas, a sub-chief of the Cayuses with whom the Doctor had always had trouble. The Doctor looked grave.

"If Tamayhas' wife dies," he said, "my life may be the forfeit. Will you go with me, Brother Spalding?"

"I'll be glad to," said Rev. Spalding. "I want to hold services at the lodge of Stikus on the Umatilla anyway. Shall we start at once?"

"Right away," said the Doctor, and after a few hurried preparations, the two were soon on their way. Mounted on their strong, fleet Cayuse horses, they rode through the night.

"I didn't want to speak of it before your family, Brother

Whitman," remarked Rev. Spalding as they rode along, but do you think there is any danger of an outbreak among the Cayuses? I have heard many rumors lately."

"I think not at present," said Dr. Whitman, "but that half-breed, Joe Lewis, is from Maine and came out here with the last emigrant train. I hear he is trying to stir up trouble. I sent him out of here with another emigrant train to get rid of him, but he came back. If the Indians were let alone I'd have no trouble with them, but if I die by the hands of the Indians, my death may do more good for Oregon than my life can." (Bancroft, the historian, said, "Dr. Whitman was a man capable of making such a remark.")

They arrived late at the lodge of Stikus, near what is now Pendleton, Oregon, thoroughly wet. They spread their blankets down by a good fire and slept soundly until morning. They ate breakfast of potatoes, squash, fresh beef, and wheat bread, all prepared by the wife of Stikus who had been trained by Mrs. Whitman.

Dr. Whitman remarked to Rev. Spalding, "How gratifying to notice the advancement of these people and their present abundance, as compared to their wretchedness and starvation when we came to them eleven years ago."

Sunday morning, Nov. 28, Dr. Whitman mounted his horse and made numerous calls on the sick at the camp of Five Crows, and Young Chief, and while there made a short call on the priests. He declined to stay for tea, saying that he had to hasten home as several children of his own were not expected to live.

Going back, he stopped again at the lodge of Stikus. As he was mounting his horse, Chief Stikus whispered to him, "Brother Whitman, the Indians have decided against you. Go away and stay until they have better hearts. The young men are very bad. They don't let the Chiefs know what they will do."

Dr. Whitman again rode through a cold and stormy night,

MOUNT HOOD FROM THE COLUMBIA RIVER

SPOTTED CAYUSE PONY

The pride of the Cayuse Indians

and towards morning arrived at his Mission to find the two Sager boys sitting up with the sick. He sent them to bed and sat up the rest of the night himself. Then, going to his wife, he told her of the warning of Stikus. "But I don't think they will kill anyone but me," he said sadly.

Mrs. Whitman was terrified.

"Oh, Marcus!" she sobbed, "I can't think of a life in this wild country without you. If you die, I want to die with you."

"But Narcissa," the Doctor soothed, "God has given us these children to raise and we must think of them. But if things do not clear up by Spring, I will move to the Willamette Valley." And then they knelt in prayer together.

Mr. Spalding stayed over a few days to hold services with the Indians at the camp of Stikus. He was pleased to note the quietness of the Indians during the Sabbath and at the appointed hour they assembled in large numbers and Mr. Spalding preached to them.

He visited other camps and returned to the lodge of Stickus Tuesday night, November 30th. That evening the chief communicated to Spalding the significant information that a decree of outlawry had been passed by the Cayuses against the white people in their country, and declined to explain any further, giving no hint of the massacre. The missionary cast himself upon his couch of skins, but sleep was impossible. On either side sat an Indian woman chanting the harsh and melancholy death song of her people. When he asked for whom they mourned, no answer could be obtained.

Early the next morning he prepared to return to Waiilatpu. At a little distance from the lodge a native woman waited. Laying her hand on the neck of his horse, she warned him in a few hurried words, to avoid Waiilatpu, site of the Whitman Mission.

Considering that his daughter Eliza was at Waiilatpu, this

information was not calculated to ease his mind or cause him to loiter; worse yet, the path from Umatilla to Waiilatpu led past the camp of Tamsucky, a fierce and cruel Indian with whom Dr. Whitman had always had difficulty. But the fearless missionary hastened on his way. Within a few miles of the Whitman Mission he met a priest with his interpreter and another Indian. Recognizing the priest as one he had met at Fort Walla Walla, he asked him if he had come from Waiilatpu and how Dr. Whitman and his family were. The priest hesitated but kept talking to the Indians in French; finally they rode on, then the priest told him of the massacre and warned him to make his escape as the Indians intended to kill him. He gave Mr. Spalding a little bread and meat he had with him. The missionary, filled with alarm, handed the ropes of his two pack horses to the priest, and turning his horse, rapidly disappeared in the gathering darkness. He had a very perilous time but reached his mission and safety.

Monday morning, November 29th, Mrs. Whitman asked the Doctor to go upstairs and see Lorinda.

Dr. Whitman went to her and reported to Mrs. Whitman, "She isn't so well and I couldn't console her. I wish you would see what you can do to comfort her. She seems terribly depressed."

Mrs. Whitman, in alarm, went to see Lorinda again.

"Lorinda, dear, don't cry so. Tell me what's troubling you," she said kindly. Lorinda burst forth into fresh sobs. "Oh, Mrs. Whitman, I dreamed such a terrible dream; I thought the Indians came and killed us all!"

"Dear child," soothed Mrs. Whitman, "You are worrying. Put your faith in Christ Jesus. I'll help you dress and come down stairs. After breakfast you will cheer up."

WAIILATPU

1. The Emigrant House where the survivors were held prisoners. 2. Flour mill. 3. Blacksmith shop. 4. The home of Marcus Whitman, where the massacre was committed. 5. Teloukike's village

LORINDA BEWLEY AT THE LODGE OF FIVE CROWS

That same morning when little Matilda came into the dining room she went to the Doctor, and putting her arms about his neck, cried, "Oh, Father! I had such a bad dream. I thought the Indians killed us all!"

He quieted her fears as best he could.

The morning passed as usual, but a small number of young men, twelve or fourteen, encouraged by the sub-chiefs, Tamayhas and Tamsucky and by several French half breeds, had gone again and again to Chief Teloukaike begging his consent to kill Dr. Whitman. Finally, in exasperation, he growled, "If you will do it, go and kill him!!"

Teloukaike was sorry as soon as he said it, but it was too late. He couldn't stop them.

Teloukaike was a proud and haughty Indian, war chief of the Cayuses and Dr. Whitman's interpreter. At this time he was angry because Dr. Whitman would not baptize him, as he thought he would receive some wonderful spiritual gift with baptism. Teloukaike had five wives and the Doctor being a strict Presbyterian had refused to baptize him until he had put all his wives away but one.

Teloukaike said, "Brother Whitman, I can't do it. My old wife, she mother my sons. I take care her. My next wife, she take care me. Three women work. I can't get along!" and he turned away in anger.

It was Monday, the first day of school, November 29th. Most of the children, save for those still convalescing from measles, were in school. Dr. Whitman's brow was serene, with no hint of the storm that raged in his breast showing in his face, although he was unusually serious. Mrs. Whitman did not come down to lunch and Elizabeth took some food on a plate and a cup of coffee and went to her room, where she found Mrs. Whitman weeping. She thanked Elizabeth for her trouble, told her to set the food on the stand, and go back downstairs. Afterwards she came down with a calm demeanor and went about with a light step attending the sick.

There was to be an Indian burial that morning, and Dr. Whitman occupied himself in reading the Bible and in talking to Mr. Rogers about the trouble that seemed to be hovering over them. Then he went to the burial, and on returning, remarked that only a few Indians, besides the relatives, attended the funeral.

PART TWO

THE MASSACRE BEGINS

About one-thirty in the afternoon, November 29, 1847, the men butchered a beef, and the Indians began to gather in large numbers.

Mrs. Whitman noticed it and asked, "Marcus, why are the Indians gathering?"

"They always do when a beef is killed," he replied, and went on reading his Bible. In the room with Mrs. Whitman and the children was Lorinda Bewley, and Catherine and Elizabeth Sager who had not yet fully recovered from the measles.

Presently an Indian rapped on the door and asked for medicine. With his Bible still in his hand, the Doctor stepped into the kitchen, where several Indians were standing about. One of these was Chief Teloukaike, and with him were his son Edward, and Tamayhas, called "The Murderer."

While Teloukaike engaged the Doctor in conversation, Tamayhas stepped behind him, drew a pipe tomahawk from beneath his blanket, and struck the Doctor in the back of the head, and following it instantly by a second blow which brought Dr. Whitman stunned, but not lifeless, to the floor.

John Sager, sitting in the room, drew his pistol but was shot by Indians who had their Hudson's Bay muskets concealed under their blankets. John fought desperately for his life, wounding in the foot, the Indian Tamayhas, the murderer of Dr. Whitman.

The shots seemed to be the signal for a general massacre.

Tamsucky and Tamayhas, sub-chiefs of the camp of Teloukaike, Edward and Clark, sons of Teloukaike, and twelve or fourteen young Indians from the camp of Tamayhas and Tamsucky living about three miles from the Mission and the half breed Joe Lewis were the only ones who took part in the massacre.

Dr. Whitman had always had trouble with these two savage sub-chiefs, and the half-breed Joe Lewis had come among them with the story that Dr. Whitman was poisoning them. There had been many deaths from the measles, with five or six being buried daily, although few of the Indians believed his story. Dr. Whitman was called upon to attend the sick up to the day of his death. He had been their doctor for eleven years and had done them much good.

Mrs. Whitman, hearing the shots, rushed to the doors, locking them, and then began to gather the children about her. The Indians did not come to these rooms, but left the kitchen to join in the dreadful destruction outside.

The first shock over, the truth flashed through the mind of Mrs. Whitman — (Catherine said, "Years later the look of speechless agony on the face of Mrs. Whitman would never fade from her mind".) She walked the floor with white cheeks and dry eyes, wringing her hands. She listened at the kitchen door; all seemed quiet. Just then Mrs. Hayes came in from another room, and with her assistance Mrs. Whitman drew her dying husband into the dining room and placed his head upon a pillow, doing all she could to stop the bleeding and revive him, but to no purpose; — the dreadful work was done. She begged him to speak to her, questioning him, but at all her questions he replied, "no," in a low voice. After receiving the first blow he was no doubt insensible.

School had begun that morning with Mr. Saunders as teacher; Eliza Spalding, Matilda Sager and Frank Sager and the children of the emigrants staying there were all in the school room. When Mr. Saunders heard the shots he stepped to the door and was attacked and killed.

Frank Sager then helped the school children to climb through a hole in the ceiling and hide in the attic, but in a short time Joe Lewis came and ordered them to come down. Frank did not come down with the others, and no doubt could have escaped — but he understood the Indian language, and hearing them say they were going to kill them all — he came down— and going to his beloved little sisterMatilda—he put his arm around her and said — "The Indians will kill me, but if you are spared, be a good girl, and meet me in heaven." The children were lined up to be shot — an Indian jerked Frank out and Joe Lewis shot him. Eliza Spalding covered her face with her apron — so she would not see them shoot her. There they stood in a long row — the young Indians leaning on their guns — waiting for the order from their chief to fire. There is pity even in the heart of a savage, and those innocent children, quietly awaiting death, moved the heart of the Chief — poor little things, how frightened they are — let us not kill them.

Little ten year old Elizabeth Sager, looking out the window cried, "Oh, Mother! They are killing the teacher!"

Elizabeth Sager was in the room with Mrs. Whitman.

Mrs. Whitman stepped to the window and looked out. A young Indian standing on the schoolhouse steps fired, the shot striking her in the breast. She sank on her knees, praying fervently to God to protect her adopted children; again to be left orphaned, and her aged Mother and Father, that they might be sustained under this terrible shock. She prayed also for the savages, for they knew not what they did. Some of them, it is said, hearing her pray for them, turned away in shame and took no further part in the massacre.

A large number of Indians were present, but the survivors said only a few were armed.

Mr. Rogers and Mr. Kimball had just come in from outside and although both were wounded, rushed to the assistance of Mrs. Whitman and carried her upstairs, where Catherine and Elizabeth had taken refuge, and where they had also carried up the sick children.

Through it all, Lorinda stayed bravely at Mrs. Whitman's side, helping her in every way she could.

The room below them began to fill with Indians who broke in the doors and windows. When they broke in the door leading up the stairs, Mr. Kimball said, "If we only had a gun we might keep them from coming up."

"There is an old gun over there in the corner," whispered Lorinda, "I'll get it."

"Give it to me," said Mr. Rogers. "I'll hold it over the stairway."

The appearance of the gun checked the Indians.

A few words passed between Mr. Rogers and one of the Indians, then turning to Mrs. Whitman he said:

"They want me to come down."

"I am afraid for you to go, Mr. Rogers," she said. "I feel we can't trust them."

"They say they are not going to kill any more," he said. "I think I had best go."

Mrs. Whitman gave him her hand saying: "The Lord bless you, go."

Mr. Rogers went down the stairs but remained in plain sight and hearing of Mrs. Whitman and Lorinda.

The Indians called to him, "You have guns and will kill us." But he replied, "No, you want to get us down to kill us." And after more conversation he called up to Mrs. Whitman:

"They say they want to come up to talk it over."

She replied: "Let just one come up, — let it be Tamsucky," not knowing that he was one of the murderers of her husband. Tamsucky came, and shaking hands with them all, professing to be very sorry.

"You must all go over to the other house," he said. "The young men are going to burn this one."

The Indians who had been yelling wildly in the room below, were gone when the party came down. They had to pass the body of Dr. Whitman on their way out. He was still breathing, but was unconscious. Upon seeing him, Mrs. Whitman became faint and was placed upon a settee. Lorinda put a pillow under Mrs. Whitman's head and a blanket over her. Lorinda walked on one side of Mrs. Whitman and Elizabeth Sager on the other. Mr. Rogers took one end of the settee and Joe Lewis, the half breed, the other. They carried her over the bodies of the Doctor and John Sager, passing through the kitchen by way of the outside door. Here, to their surprise, they found the Indians collected, guns ready. Elizabeth saw the Indians lined up with guns pointed, and turning, ran back upstairs.

When the settee had gone but its length from the door, Joe Lewis dropped his end of it.

Immediately the young Indians fired.

Mr. Rogers had only time to raise his hands and gasp, "Oh! My God! Save me!" and sank to the ground dead.

Mrs. Whitman received another wound and died later in the night. She lay all night on the muddy ground. — Next day some of the Indian women lifted her onto the wood pile and covered her with a blanket.

Turning quickly, Lorinda saw Joe Lewis draw his pistol and shoot Frank Sager. Terrified at the fiendish shouting of the Indians, she ran screaming toward the emigrant house; but an Indian soon overtook her, shaking his tomahawk over her head, but she kept on screaming until others came running up, pointing their guns at her threatening her with tomahawks, until she finally understood they wanted her to hush. When she was silent, Tamsucky took her by the hand and led her over to the emigrant house, where the survivors were prisoners. Tamsucky was planning to take Lorinda for his wife.

It was now getting dark and there appeared on the scene, Beardy, an influential sub-chief and convert of Dr. Whitman, who made an eloquent plea for the lives of the women and children.

Teloukaike, the War Chief, called to the women to come and take their children over to the emigrant house. They rushed to gather up their little ones to take them, (these were the children that were in school), but in the excitement forgot little Matilda Sager and Eliza Spalding, who were left standing among the dead, grasping each other's hands, too terrified to move. They were seen by the old Indian Chief Stickus, faithful friend of Dr. Whitman, who went to them taking them kindly by the hand and led them over to the emigrant house; giving them into the care of Mrs. Saunders, who made them a bed on the floor. They were so exhausted that they immediately went to sleep and slept soundly until morning.

That night, Catherine and Elizabeth , with the sick children, little Henrietta, Hannah Louise, Helen Mar Meek and the wounded man, Mr. Kimball, stayed upstairs in the Doctor's house. They heard the clock in the room below strike every hour —and it tolled the midnight hour before those wounded breathed their last.

Elizabeth could never, during her life time, bear to hear a clock strike. She never had one in her home.

They did not know but what they were the only ones left alive. Towards morning the sick children began calling for water. Catherine asked Elizabeth to go down to the kitchen and get a bucket of water that was sitting on a bench. Elizabeth got up enough courage to go down but she was so frightened she turned the bucket of water over, so had to go back without any.

Day began to break, and Mr. Kimball told Catherine to

take a sheet off the bed and bind up his arm and he would try and get some water. She said, "Mother would not like her sheets to be torn up." Looking at her he said, "Child, don't you know that your mother is dead and will never have any use for her sheets." Finally she took a sheet and bound up his arm. He wrapped a blanket around himself, Catherine placed his hat on his head and he went out. They waited long for him but he did not return, and they never saw him alive again.

The children begged so piteously for water, Elizabeth went down again to get it. Young Edward, Teloukaike's son, was in the kitchen and she asked him to get some water for her. He went out and brought her a bucket full. While he was gone, she went through the house, opening door after door. She looked at Dr. Whitman, who lay with his eyes wide open. There were two mutilations across his nose, but nothing else. Finally, she saw the body of her brother, Frank, lying near the door of the Indian room. She then turned and went back up stairs and told her sister Catherine that their brother Frank was killed. The Indians had told them that he had escaped. (Frank hid in the attic and could have made his escape, but he heard the Indians say they were going to kill them all and he came down saying he did not wish to live if the rest were killed.)

A little later they heard the Indians gathering in the room below. Teloukaike called for them to come down and go over to the emigrant house with the other survivors, as they were going to burn the Mission, and that no more were to be killed.

Catherine told Elizabeth to go over to the emigrant house and get help to carry the sick children. As she started out, she met Lorinda with Mary Ann Bridger and Helen Saunders, who helped them. Lorinda came to see if her brother Crockett was yet alive. She was overjoyed to find he had been overlooked by the murderers. (Crockett and Mr. Sales were in a small bed room.) Crockett was very ill with measles. He was moved over to the emigrant house. Lorinda helped carry the children over. Catherine and Elizabeth went through Mrs.

Whitman's room and found it full of Indian women gathering Mrs. Whitman's clothes and crying as though their hearts would break.

They cried harder when they saw the poor frightened children and loaded Elizabeth down with Mrs. Whitman's dresses. Elizabeth grasped them in her arms and held them tight. Later she took them down to Oregon City with her. After she was married she wanted to preserve them, and the only way she knew how was to make them into quilts. So, she made three; one for herself, one for Catherine, and one for Matilda. One of these is now in existence in Eugene, Oregon, at the home of Mrs. Bertha Doris, daughter of Matilda.

As they neared the emigrant house, Mrs. Saunders, the wife of the teacher, met them and kissed them and said, "The Indians have promised not to kill any more. Your dear mother is dead and I will try and be a mother to you." This she faithfully did.

The night of the massacre, the Indians held a Council in the lodge of the half breed Finley to decide the fate of the prisoners. Many eloquent speeches were made in their favor.

Tamsucky got up and said, "The best thing to do is to kill them all." But he was met by such a scathing rebuke, he sat down and said no more. They finally came to no definite decision. The lodge where they met was but a short distance from the emigrant house.

Mrs. Saunders, the wife of the teacher, accompanied by Chief Stikus, went to the lodge and waited outside until Chief Teloukaike came out. She pleaded for the lives of the women and children saying, "They have never harmed him. That they would work and sew for the Indians if he would spare their lives." He said, "No, you no harm the Indians, women and children shall not be killed while I live. Tamsucky very bad man, you must be careful not to make some of the Indians mad; they want excuse to kill. Me very sad about Dr. Whitman, he our best friend. Indians will now become like they were before he come. No one to tell them of the better way to live — the way of the Man on the Cross. I do not care to live. I would give my life for the safety of my people. The Great Spirit will hide his face; much weeping is heard in the wigwams."

Elizabeth said, "Mrs. Saunders never seemed afraid of the Indians; she always sent the children for Teloukaike if some Indian got too overbearing."

On Tuesday the day after the massacre, a young artist, J. H. Stanley, was on his way with an Indian guide to the Whitman Mission to paint pictures of the Indians. When near the Mission he met a friendly Indian who told him of the massacre and advised him to go to Fort Walla Walla.

When the first shots were heard, Mr. Osborn, one of the emigrants, raised a board in the floor of their room in the Doctor's house, where an excavation had been started, and here they found room to secrete themselves until about midnight, when Mr. Osborn took his family with him and made his escape. Mrs. Osborn was not well and she gave out after a few miles, and Mr. Osborn hid his family in the trees and bushes along the river, and taking his youngest child made his way to Fort Walla Walla. Mr. Osborn said that McBain refused to help him bring his family to the Fort.

Fortunately Mr. Stanley had arrived at the Fort, and he gave Mr. Osborn what food he had, his horses, and best of all his trusty Spokane Indian guide to go back and get his family.

When arriving near the place where Mrs. Osborn and family had been left, he could not find them. He almost gave up, but the Indian wouldn't quit hunting, and at last found them almost perished from hunger and cold.

They put Mrs. Osborn on behind the Indian and tied her to him. Mr. Osborn carried the children.

Mr. Osborn said that the half breed McBain, in charge of Fort Walla Walla, refused to take them in, and told them to go to the Umatillas. Mrs. Osborn refused to go — McBain finally received them into the Fort and put them in a secret room. He wanted Mr. Osborn to go down the Columbia, but he refused.

IN CAPTIVITY

THE prisoners were all moved to the emigrant house, a large two-story building, the lower floor divided into four rooms, and three large and two small ones on the upper floor. When Catherine reached the house she fainted. As soon as she recovered she said, "I must go back and get Helen (Helen Marr Meek), she is there all alone." Catherine and Lorinda went back after her — she was conscious and screaming — almost frightened to death. She thought they had deserted her. Now the house was left to the dead. None went back that day. It was crowded with Indians looting and destroying everything — emptying bed ticks and scattering the feathers.

Elizabeth said that after the second day she went over several times each day, but she could not bear to touch anything. They were now all held as prisoners in the Emigrant House.

Mrs. Saunders, wife of the teacher, and five children, occupied two large rooms on the first floor, took the Whitman children and Eliza Spalding in with her. Lorinda Bewley helped her with them. Mrs. Nathan Kimball and four children, Mrs. Peter Hall and five children, the widow Rebecca Hays and her young son, Mrs. Canfield and four children, little Mary Marsh, whose father was killed, Catherine, Elizabeth, Matilda and Henrietta Sager and Lorinda Bewley, were all with Mrs. Saunders.

Teloukaike had lived near Dr. Whitman for eleven years and was fairly well civilized. His camp was just across the road; he did not want the prisoners mistreated.

The day after the massacre, the women got consent of the chiefs to bury the dead. Joe Stanfield dug a long shallow grave and the next day, Wednesday, the women and children sewed sheets around the corpses and prepared them the best they could for burial.

That morning the Indians came to the emigrant house and told the women to get dinner for the Priest, that he was at the lodge of Teloukaike and would come and help bury the dead. Elizabeth said he came, and ate his dinner and had nothing to say to them.

Now their life as captives of the Indians began. They were told that they would hold them until Spring and if the Americans did not come to rescue them they would send them down to the Willamette Valley, but if they heard that the Americans were coming they would kill them all. This kept them in constant fear.

Chief Teloukaike made the Indians return to the prisoners a great many of the things they had taken. The Indian women would come in with shoes and other things they had taken.

One day Edward came in with his arms loaded with clothes and asked that all of Dr. Whitman's children come to him and he distributed the things among them. At another time an Indian came in and gave Catherine a bucket of syrup and a pocket compass that had belonged to Dr. Whitman.

The Indians provided them with plenty of food from the Doctor's supplies, both meat and vegetables, and all of the stock of sugar.

Every morning early, the Indians who had taken part in the massacre, would come from their camp a few miles away, and the prisoners had to cook for them. They were very suspicious of them and made the women eat of the food before they ate, — afraid of being poisoned. They stayed until late at night. Often they would stretch themselves out on the beds and their prisoners would have to sit up until they left.

The Indian women seldom came to the emigrant house. The prisoners lived from day to day, never knowing when they would be killed.

On the 5th of December, little Hannah Louisa, six years old, died of the measles. Dr. Whitman did not expect Hannah Louisa or Helen Marr Meek to recover, and three days after the death of Hannah Louisa, Helen Marr Meek also died.

The Indians kept the women busy working for them. They brought a bolt of yellow flannel from the Mission House for the women to make up into shirts for them. An Indian was very angry at one time because he said the sewing was not good, and would pull out. Mrs. Saunders convinced him they were doing the best they could. All of them had to knit socks and leggings for the Indians.

Mr. Sales and Crocket Bewley were recovering rapidly and were now sitting up most of the time. The Indians told them they would have to take squaw wives and live among the Indians. Crocket Bewley would make no reply, but young Sales who hated them bitterly, would curse them and said he would do no such thing, but as soon as he was well enough he was going down to the Willamette Valley.

Dr. Whitman had never allowed the Indians to learn to run the flour mill, so the Indians decided to bring down the two families at the saw mill. Mr. Young and family, and Mr. Smith and family were camped at Dr. Whitman's sawmill in the edge of the Blue Mountains getting out lumber. Not knowing anything of the massacre, a son of Elem Young started down to the Mission with a load of lumber and was met and killed by the Indians. In a few days his brother came down horseback to see what had happened to him, as he had not returned. The Indians went up the next day and brought back the two families, and they were moved in with the other prisoners in the Emigrant House.

Eliza Spalding was the only one that could speak the Nez Perces' language and she was called upon to interpret for the Indians until she was completely exhausted, and her grief over the supposed death of her father and mother caused her to take a fever and she lay between life and death for days. One day two trusted Nez Perce Indians came for Eliza — bringing word that her father and mother were alive and under the protection of their faithful Nez Perces. They also brought a letter from Mr. Canfield to his wife — telling her of his escape and arrival at the Spalding Mission.

The Cayuses would not let them take Eliza — told them if they tried to take her they would kill her. Eliza wept — Chief Timothy wiped her eyes with her apron and said "Don't cry, Eliza, you shall see your mother."

Before Mr. Smith and Mr. Young arrived the women were dependent on Joe Stanfield to get the wood for the stoves. This service he performed so grudgingly that they felt they would rather go without than ask him. He dealt out their provisions to them and did it to suit himself — his favorite among them faring best. This was the cause of some hard feelings. He had known of the massacre three days before it happened. When asked why he did not let it be known, he replied, "It would have done no good."

He had fallen in love with Mrs. Hays, and had told the Indians that she was his wife — and she must make the Indians think so. She consented to this to help save the lives of the rest. He now tried to get her to elope with him some night. This she steadfastly refused to do, asking him what would become of the rest if she deserted them. He replied, "Let them go to hell."

It was the custom of the prisoners to gather in some one of the rooms to spend the evening. They felt better to be together. One evening Catherine was sitting by the fire in a room some distance from the one she occupied, when a stalwart savage came in, seized her by the arm and dragged her shrieking through the house to another room, which was empty at that time, excepting for the sleeping children. Placing a chair, he told her to sit down. He then began to court her for his friend. The friend soon came in and she was forced to listen to their love speeches. Joe Stanfield soon came in and told them not to try to carry her away. They said they did not want, or intend to; they only wanted to amuse themselves. She could not see the fun, but sat shivering with fright and cold. She begged them to let her go to the fire; they refused, and wrapped a blanket around her. They made her life a torment to her. She was so afraid of being carried off by them that she was tempted to end her troubles by jumping into the mill pond. A few nights after she found a place to hide and they didn't find her. They went out, giving vent to their chagrin in loud whoops.

Soon after the Indians came again. Catherine was in bed asleep. She felt someone pulling her by the arm. Starting up she saw him. He wanted her to sit by the fire with him; she refused. He tried coaxing and threats, but in her desperation she lost all fear of him and fought with teeth and nails.

He told her if she would sit and talk with him, he would go away, but she would not. She told him that she hated him.

The contest lasted for sometime, then he raised his whip and said he would whip her, but she cared not, and still fought him, calling upon the other Indians that were sleeping near to help her, but they paid no heed.

Joe Stanfield getting tired of the row jumped up and called on the white men to help him drive that "dam Injun" out.

He then left and never came back.

The Indians called her a brave girl, that would thus fight a man.

Knowing how treacherous the nature of savages was, they lived in constant fear of being murdered. They watched for the coming of the Indians in the morning and only felt safe after they departed at night.

It was Catherine's custom to take her little sister Henrietta, three years old and just rcovering from a long and severe illness, in her arms and sit down on the floor behind the stove every morning and await the coming of the Indians, resolving to die with her in her arms if they murdered them.

Occasionally she would go over to her desolated home. What a scene presented itself there — mutilated furniture, feathers, ashes, straw and blood. Desolation reigned where once had been peace and harmony.

Amid all the anguish and turmoil of those dark days there would sometimes occur things that were ludicrous enough to make them for a moment forget their sorrow and indulge in a hearty laugh.

One day an Indian brave came riding up to the house with a large map of the world, thrown over his horse for a blanket.

At another time the voices of the children would be heard — singing hymns, accompanied by the Indians — Oh, blessed childhood that can thus throw off sorrow and gloom.

The leader of the twelve or fourteen young Indians who took an active part in the massacre was Istulest—a savage and cruel young Indian. He would come late at night after the other Indians had gone home and succeeded in frightening them all.

Chief Beardy came often in the daytime, to visit the prisoners. The women told him these young renegades came and frightened the children — so Chief Beardy agreed to stay to protect them. The women would always set him a lunch before he left. One night they made dried peach pie — he ate so heartily of it that it made him very sick. He stayed away two days — on the third day he rode up with a bunch of his men. He was furiously angry and told them he was going to kill them all, that he had saved their lives, and now they had poisoned him. In vain the women tried to explain. Fortunately an Indian woman named Catherine, who had lived in Dr. Whitman's family, and had married a white man, and lived near Fort Hall, had arrived that morning. As soon as she heard of the massacre she rode day and night and arrived just in time. Elizabeth said she got down on her knees in front of Chief Beardy and pleaded for their lives, and she finally convinced him that he had only eaten too much. After that he would laugh heartily when peach pie was mentioned.

The Indian woman spoke good English. She told them that as soon as the educated young Chief Ellis, head Chief of the Nez Perces returned from the Buffalo hunt he would set them free. He never returned; He and most of his men died in the Buffalo country.

Crocket Bewley improved rapidly and one day, about a week after the massacre, he said to his sister, "Lorinda, I am afraid Tamsucky means to take you away for his wife, but I'll soon be well enough to make my escape and get down to the Willamette Valley to bring help."

"Brother, you are still too weak to go," she said. "And besides if you attempted to leave now the Indians would kill you."

"I care nothing for my life," said Crocket. "If I can deliver you from this terrible captivity."

"Careful, Crocket," she whispered. "Joe Lewis and Joe Stanfield are listening." And when, a few days later her brother and young Sales were killed, she was convinced that they had heard.

Chief Teloukaike was worried about the safety of the white prisoners. The young murderers were clamoring for his consent to take the young white girls for their wives. He refused, but was afraid he could not control them. He knew he should always be sorry he gave his consent to kill Dr. Whitman.

In the Councils they could come to no settlement. He must consult Five Crows. He sent his son Edward, mounted on a swift horse, to the Umatillas to ask the advice of Five Crows.

Late that evening, Edward sprang from his foaming horse

at the lodge of Five Crows, and slipping through the door of the lodge, he stood like a bronze statue.

Five Crows leaped to his feet.

"What is the matter?" he demanded. "Why do you stand there?"

"Dr. Whitman is dead!" gasped Edward.

"Who killed him? Answer me! you dog!" thundered the Chief.

"Some young men from the camp of my father, Teloukaike," answered the young man.

Five Crows frowned. "Can't Teloukaike control his young men? — Is he old? — Has he no more strength? Deliver those murderers to me and I will punish them like the dogs they are."

"How many were there?" he stormed.

"Only a few, twelve or fourteen, led by the half breed Joe Lewis," said Edward.

"What about Mrs. Whitman?" demanded the Chief.

"She is dead too, and most of the men," said Edward.

"Where are the women and children?" demanded the Chief.

"They are held prisoners in the emigrant house," was the answer.

Five Crows was furious!

"Oh! You Fools! Have you no brains?" he stormed. "You have killed the best friends the Indians will ever have. This will bring a war with the Americans."

"Joe Lewis said the Hudson's Bay Company would not let the Boston men punish us," said Edward.

"I tell you to go back to Teloukaike and tell him there will be no more white people killed. I, Chief Five Crows, will hold him responsible."

Suddenly he stopped.

"Where is the golden haired girl?" he demanded.

"Chief Teloukaike said for you to take her for a wife, if you promise to help, if we have trouble with the Americans," replied Edward. "He is afraid the bad ones of our tribe will steal her when he is not near."

Five Crows' heart leaped, the fire died out of his eyes.

"Get a fresh horse and ride back tonight," he said.

"Tomorrow, I will send for the white girl."

In a few minutes Edward was speeding over the hills and arrived at the emigrant house the next afternoon. He immediately went to the room where Crocket Bewley and Mr. Sales were and gave the signal for the young Indians to kill them, which they did in a most brutal manner, then threw their bodies out of doors, where they lay for two days. Lorinda went upstairs and hid herself under the bed in one of the small bedrooms and gave vent to her grief. The Indians were anxious to know where she was and if she cared for her brothers' death. The prisoners pretended not to know where she was or if she cared.

The next day word came from Fort Walla Walla that no more Americans were to be killed, and if they were the Hudson Bay Company would join the Americans and punish them. But it came too late to save these two young men.

That same day two Indians rode in leading a horse. Eliza Spalding looking from the window, cried: "There is my horse, Tasche. Now I know my father is killed for he had my horse with him."

One of the Indians entered the room, and pointing to Lorinda, said, "Me take that white squaw to Umatilla to Five Crows' lodge. Hurry, Hurry!" Lorinda, clasping her hand to her breast, sank to her knees. This burden seemed too much for her to bear.

"Children," said Mrs. Saunders, "run and tell Teloukaike to come over and tell us what to do."

In a few minutes he came from his lodge, which was a short distance from the Doctor's house. He seemed much relieved to have Lorinda taken to Five Crows. "Many young men very bad," he said. "Tamsucky bad, all time want to take white girl to his lodge. I say no. Five Crows all same white man. He be good to white girl."

While the women wept with Lorinda, they thought, too, that she would be safer away from the Mission. Wrapping her as best they could from their scanty supply of blankets she was lifted to a horse, too ill and grief stricken to make any resistance. The Indians tied her securely, and leading her horse, they rode away into the gathering dusk of the cold December day. Turning for a last look at the Mission vanishing in the distance, Lorinda thought her heart would break. To leave her dear brother, murdered and unburied, perhaps never to see her dear mother and father or any white people again, doomed to live out her life among savages, seemed unbearable. She sent up a fervent prayer, "Oh, God, send me help or let me die."

The Indians found a camping place, built a fire and cooked food for her, but she could not eat. That night, she lay on the frozen ground with but scanty covering, never closing her eyes, but the Indians, rolled in their blankets were soon asleep.

Snow began falling, and chilling winds blew fiercely.

Poor Lorinda thought that God and nature were combined against her. Next morning, again tied upon her horse, they continued their journey and arrived at the lodge of Five Crows about noon.

The Chief came out to meet her and lifting her tenderly from her horse, carried her into his lodge. Spreading down costly furs and robes, he laid her upon them, covering her with warm blankets. Clapping his hands he called his old slave "Sal-alle," commanding her in his native tongue:

"Get hot rocks quick! and warm her feet. Put dry clothes on her."

The old woman looked in wonder at the beautiful white girl, touching her pale skin and golden hair reverently, talking to her in a soft, soothing voice.

Although not able to understand a word that was said, the kind tone and soothing touch of the motherly old woman quieted Lorinda's fears until she fell asleep. When she awakened, Five Crows had a good fire burning and had prepared several kinds of food for her with his own hands, the greatest honor a Chief can pay a guest. Kneeling by her couch, he urged her to eat, but she turned from him in fear.

Stroking her long golden hair, he said:

"Do not fear me, little 'Snow Bird' that has come to me out of the storm, wounded and frightened; you shall be protected in the lodge of Five Crows; I will not harm you."

Her grief and helplessness moved him to unwonted tenderness; the proud and haughty Cayuse Chief had indeed become her slave.

"When I first saw you on the trail," he said, "my heart leaped within me. I have thought of you by day, and dreamed of you by night. When I look at the sunshine I think of your hair. When I behold the blue sky, I see your eyes."

Pleading with her with all an Indian's eloquence, he told her she need not decide at once to be his wife, saying, "Brother Spalding has escaped and is at his Mission. He will marry us, I am sure. It is only a day's ride. I will take you there if you will promise to marry me."

Lorinda had saved very little clothing. Five Crows gave her a beautiful doeskin dress, tanned to a light cream color, and a beautifully beaded belt and moccasins. When he saw her, her hair braided in two long braids, dressed as an Indian woman, he was more in love than before with his beautiful white squaw.

The long days and nights on the trail — the horror of the massacre and the terror that followed it — the cold and exposure — together with the fear of the Indians on the trip to the lodge of Five Crows, had brought on a return of the fever and Lorinda lay for days, scarcely conscious, tenderly nursed by the old woman and the Chief.

She slowly regained her strength but was so sad and heart broken, Five Crows tried in every way to cheer her up. Finally he told her she could go over to the house of the white men, the Catholic Priests, that had moved into a three roomed cabin about one-half mile from the lodge of Five Crows and he would come for her in the evening.

When he came she refused to go back with him. He turned and strode haughtily out. The priests seemed greatly alarmed and told her she had better go. She said she would rather die. Finally they ordered one of the Indians to take her over to Five Crows' lodge. He pushed her inside the door. Five Crows was sitting before the fire with his head in his hands. He looked up and said, "If you don't want to marry me, you don't have to. Go back to the white men's house and I won't bother you."

She hurriedly gathered her scanty belongings and went back to the priests' house. They treated her kindly but in a few days Five Crows again came and took her by force back to his lodge.

The next evening two Nez Perce Chiefs, James and Red Wolf brought news that Mr. Spalding had escaped and was making every effort to have the prisoners rescued. Although she scarcely dared hope, the thought of escape gave Lorinda a ray of comfort.

Two days after Lorinda Bewley was taken to the Umatilla, the Indians held a Council at the emigrant house and requested that all prisoners be present. A Chief got up and made a speech to them, pointing out their helpless condition, and that they

Although the Indians would joke about it, they kept their distance.

Meanwhile, Edward, being the eldest son of Teloukaike had usurped most of the old Chief's authority, and Teloukaike had lost much of his influence. Edward was a handsome young Indian, his color being lighter than most. He was always gentlemanly in his treatment of the prisoners, but still he was an Indian.

He had taken an active part in the massacre, and now wore the clothes of John Sager. He was becoming greatly attracted to Mary Smith, and she was just the type of girl to attract the attention of a young brave. Her figure was small and slender, her eyes flashing and dark, and her hair black and curly. After his brother gave her up he turned his thoughts toward her.

He came to Catherine one evening to talk it over. He said he would like her for a wife, but that she was too young, being only twelve years old. He said, if she was his girl he would not leave her. Catherine told him to ask Mary if he wanted to, and she had reasons afterwards to regret throwing off his protection.

Edward told Mary that if she would marry him, he would protect her and her family. She talked it over with her father and mother, and they agreed that this was the only way to save their lives, and perhaps through Edward, save the lives of the others.

Edward then called a Council of his people and declared his intention of taking Mary Smith for his wife, as his brother Clark had given her up. Mary was a brave girl, and made the most of the situation, using her influence over him to gain protection for her own family and all the other captives. When in his presence she appeared cheerful and contented, but Catherine said when she was away from him, Mary would weep and moan as though her heart would break.

Never was a bridegroom prouder of his wife than Edward was of his handsome white girl. He would come in and inquire,

"Where is my wife?" with such an air of importance, as to draw a smile from the faces of the beholders. He now applied himself to the study of English with greater earnestness than ever.

Mary had great influence over him, and this she used to good advantage, telling him her father was an Englishman, and a man of great importance. This caused the Indians to treat him with great respect, and, of course, gained protection for him in case of another massacre.

Several days after the massacre Mr. McBain sent a Frenchman down to Fort Vancouver with a letter reporting the massacre at the Whitman Mission.

The messenger stopped at The Dalles Mission, and asked Mr. Hinman, who was in charge, to help him get a canoe to continue his journey to Vancouver. Mr. Hinman decided to go to Vancouver with the messenger. When they got below the Cascades the messenger then told Hinman of the massacre of Dr. and Mrs. Whitman, and the others, at Waiilatpu. The messenger said that McBain had told him not to warn them at The Dalles.

Mr. Hinman was frantic at the thought of his family and the others being at the mercy of the Indians. When they arrived at Fort Vancouver, Mr. Hinman went with the messenger and delivered the letter to Peter Skeen Ogden, who was shocked and immediately went to Mr. Douglas, showing him the letter and saying, "Mr. Douglas, you see now what opposition in religion does!"

After a moment's pause, Mr. Douglas said, "There may be other causes."

Mr. Ogden immediately selected a large amount of Indian trading goods, and early next morning started for Fort Walla Walla with three large bateaus, each rowed by eight expert French Canadian oarsmen, and arrived at Fort Walla Walla December 19th. Mr. Hinman accompanied him as far as The

Dalles and at once removed his family and others to the Willamette Valley, leaving only a few trusted Indians in charge.

On December 20th, word was received at the Umatilla that Peter Skeen Ogden, Chief of the Hudson's Bay Company at Vancouver, had arrived at Fort Walla Walla, with Indian trading goods to redeem the captives, and that he had sent for the Chiefs and principal men to meet with him in Council.

There was great excitement among the Indians. Catching their fleetest horses, the Chiefs and most influential men dashed away to the Fort, but Five Crows did not go. He sent his brother, Young Chief, Ta-Wa-T-We, instead. Five Crows had no wish to let Lorinda go, and he thought he could still win her love. He cared nothing for the ransom offered for her release. He was a rich man, and had everything he wanted, except Lorinda. He told Young Chief to put the price so high they couldn't buy her!

The Council continued for about ten days, during which time all the prisoners, save Lorinda, were ransomed. Young Chief, knowing his brothers wish to keep Lorinda, kept putting the price higher and higher. At last Mr. Ogden said, "All or none! I must have them all!" And so Young Chief agreed to give her up.

Lorinda was frantic with joy as it became nearer a reality that escape from her captor was near. She watched every motion of the trees, the birds and the Indians. Every hour seemed a week. She scarcely ate or slept, but frequently walked to a little hill near the lodge to gaze anxiously in the direction of the Fort, hoping to see a messenger coming.

Early on the morning of December 26, the Chiefs returned from the Council, accompanied by an Indian leading a horse. He handed Lorinda a note from Peter Skeen Ogden, stating the joyful news that he had finally succeeded in redeeming all the unfortunate captives, and that she had nothing to fear, but to accompany the Indian in as fast time as possible to Fort

Walla Walla. She could scarcely believe her eyes. Joyfully she sank upon her knees, and with a grateful heart, gave thanks to God for His great mercy.

Five Crows sprang to her side, again pleading with her not to leave him. "If you will stay with me and be my wife," he begged, "I will be the greatest Chief in all the Oregon country. You shall never work as Indian women do. I have many slaves, and thousands of my cattle and horses roam the hills. You have only to wish for a thing and it shall be yours. I had nothing to do with the murder of your people. The Indians knew better than to let me know of their intentions. The guilty ones shall be punished. You shall sit in the Councils with the Chiefs, and there shall be peace between your people and my people."

"But I cannot live among the Indians," said Lorinda, "I am a white woman."

"Then," declared the Chief, "I will go with you and live among your people."

"No, Five Crows," said Lorinda, "there is a young man that came with our wagon train who is waiting for me in the Willamette Valley."

Five Crows was desperate with despair.

"Then," quoth he sadly, "There will be no more sunshine in the lodge of Five Crows. I will be alone always and when the wolf howls upon the hill he will be no more lonely than I."

"Five Crows will walk alone until he dies. No wife, no children to greet me when I return from the hunt. Only the memory of the golden hair and eyes like the sky, voice like the running brook, and fleet as the wild fawn to run from me,"

But Lorinda hurriedly packed her little bundle of clothing, giving no heed to his pleadings.

The Chief then prepared a good breakfast for her and spreading a new blanket and a buffalo robe on her saddle to

FIVE CROWS

PORTRAIT OF THE WRITER, MYRA SAGER HELM

make her comfortable during the long cold ride, he assisted her upon her horse and wrapped her in a thick warm shawl. He gave her a package of food for her journey, and bade her a reluctant, but kindly goodby.

Again Lorinda was riding with an Indian over the prairie to Fort Walla Walla.

Although more fit for a sickbed than a horseback journey of fifty-five miles on that cold winter day, she was so thrilled at her escape from a life among the savages, that with her heart singing with joy, she urged her horse into a gallop, thankful that it was a gentle and easy-riding mount. The day was cold and foggy, but thanks to Five Crows, Lorinda was warm and comfortable.

Toward evening, the Indian found a sheltered camping place, and soon had a good fire going, which he replenished several times during the night. At dawn the Indian was up. built another roaring fire, brought in the horses which he had hobbled the night before and turned out to graze. He took great pains to prepare her a nice breakfast, making tea for her in a cup which he had with him. Just before starting, he knelt down and worshipped in his native tongue. Although she could not understand a word, Lorinda knelt with him.

After breakfast, he saddled her horse, helped her on it, arranged the blankets and robes, and they were again on their way. When they came in sight of the Fort, the Indian pointed to it and said. "House suyapu aiat," meaning American woman. They rode on to the Fort and were greeted by Mr. Ogden, Mr. McBain, several Catholic priests and halfbreeds who rushed out to meet her. Mr. Ogden took her gently from her horse, saying, "Thank God, I have you safe at last. I had to pay the Indians more for you than for all the other captives. I had begun to fear they would never give you up!"

Lorinda was also greeted by Mr. Osborn and family, who had taken refuge at the fort. When word was received at Waiilatpu that three boats had arrived at Fort Walla Walla, there was great excitement among the Indians. They thought it was the Americans come to fight them, and immediately sent a messenger to find out. The messenger returned the next morning, saying it was Uncle Pete (Peter Skeen Ogden), who wanted all the Chiefs and principal men to meet with him in Council at Fort Walla Walla. The Indians all hurried away to the Fort, and after ten days, all the prisoners were ransomed.

During this time the prisoners scarcely slept, but gathered in one of the rooms. Runners kept coming from Fort Walla Walla shouting the news, and then going on back to the Fort or to the Umatilla.

When the Indians had all gathered at the Fort, Mr. Ogden made a speech to them in the Indian language, saying, "When I return I will see what can be done for you, but I do not promise to prevent war. I will pay the ransom, that is all!"

Teloukaike replied, "Your words are weighty. Your hairs are grey. We have known you a long time. I cannot therefore keep the captives back. I make them over to you, which I would not do to another younger than yourself!"

Nevertheless, Mr. Ogden argued and reasoned with the Indians many hours before all of them would agree to deliver up the captives. The ransom was paid on January 3rd, 1848, after all the prisoners were delivered to Mr. Ogden at Fort Walla Walla. During this time the prisoners at Waiilatpu had the place mostly to themselves. All those that had taken part in the massacre were at the Fort, and only a few friendly Indians were left.

Christmas Day, 1847, dawned cold and dreary and Mrs. Saunders, looking at the pale faces of the children, said to the other women, "Can't we do something to celebrate Christmas, and bring a little cheer to these poor children?"

The women cooked many dainties and decorated a cake. They also looked up the children's soiled and broken dolls and fixed them up as best they could. They set the table in one of the upper rooms and ate in secret, fearing the return of the Indians from the Fort. Although it cheered them some, they could not help but compare it with other Christmas Days at their happy homes. No singing of hymns led by the sweet voice of Narcissa Whitman.

On the night of December 26th, the prisoners were all gathered in one of the lower rooms of the emigrant house, praying and singing hymns. They were singing, "I Know That My Redeemer Liveth," when they heard a runner coming very fast. When he got to the door he shouted, "Good news! Good news!!"

Catherine Sager opened the door, and he handed her a note from Peter Ogden, saying that all the unfortuate captives had been ransomed, and for them to grind enough flour to last them the voyage down the river.

The Indians returned the next day in high spirits. They had made a treaty with Uncle Pete and sold the prisoners to him. They were to deliver them at the Fort in three days and get their pay.

Clark was especially in amazing good humor. He laughed and talked, and played tricks on the children. He told Catherine that Mr. Ogden had bought them all but her, having given her to him, and laughed heartily when she told him they would settle that at the Fort. The rescued spent all that night packing and preparing for their start for the Fort.

Edward was trying hard to get Mary Smith to remain with him, offering her great riches. She told him, "If he loved her so much to go with her."

Edward said sadly, "White man shoot me if I go with you!"

The rescued started for the Fort just at daylight, and all of them wept as they drove away from that scene of suffering —

wept for joy at their deliverance, and wept for sorrow for those that had been slain and could not join them. As they left an Indian woman from a lodge nearby told them to hasten for their lives, that her people had repented, and were going to kill them.

Joe Stanfield drove up the oxen. He hitched the best team of oxen to his wagon and Mrs. Hayes and the Smith family rode with him. They arrived about an hour ahead of the other wagons and families, as the rest were heavily loaded and the roads were muddy.

In the last wagon were the four Sager girls, Eliza Spalding, Mrs. Saunders and her family, Mary Marsh, and Eleum Young and his family. Eleum Young was the driver of this team. The morning was cold and bleak, but the thought of rescue kept their spirits high. Their team of oxen were lazy and slow, and the other wagons were far ahead.

Chief Stickus rode on one side of their team and Chief Beardy on the other. When they got on a downhill slope, they whipped the old oxen into a run. There was still fear that the Indians would change their minds if they heard the Americans were coming. They seemed to expect it.

The Tuscha River was flooded and they got very wet in crossing. The night set in cold and foggy, and they were glad at heart when they sighted the Fort in the distance.

At the Fort they were welcomed by Mr. Ogden and the others, and were overjoyed to find Lorinda there. Peter Skeen Ogden said he never closed his eyes for two nights while waiting for the prisoners to be brought in, and it is said this ordeal turned his hair snow white. He surely perfomed a great and noble deed. No other man in the country had as much influence with the Indians and could have rescued the prisoners.

PART THREE

AT THE FORT

THE rescued were taken inside the Fort and seated by a big fire and immediately served with hot food. They were then shown to their rooms and told to stay inside and not open their doors to anyone.

The men were sitting or standing around the big fireplace. The little Sager girls, peeking out of a crack in the door, were anxious to know which one was "Uncle Pete," as the Indians called him. Finally ten year old Elizabeth could restrain her curiosity no longer. Slipping out of the door, she walked up to one of the men and asked, "Which one of you is Uncle Pete?" The men laughed heartily, and after that she was a great favorite with Mr. Ogden.*

While at the Fort the women engaged themselves in baking bread for their long trip down the river in an oven outside the Fort. Mrs. Hayes and Mrs. Hall were carrying a large basket between them when Joe Stanfield came and insisted on speaking privately with Mrs. Hayes.

She told him if he had anything to say, to say it, and then he asked her to marry him.

Mrs. Hayes' eyes flashed as she replied, "No, not you or any

---

*Mr. Stanley made an oil painting of this scene after he got to Oregon City, and it is stored, with other paintings of his, in Washington, D. C.

other man! My husband has been dead but a short time. He died on the plains. And I wouldn't marry you anyway!"

Stanfield turned away, saying, "If I had known that, you could have all gone to Hell long ago!"

The survivors were waiting now for the arrival of Mr. Spalding and family. Mr. Ogden was very anxious, for he knew how determined the Cayuse Indians were to kill Mr. Spalding. At last, on Saturday morning, January 1st, a messenger brought news that they were nearing the fort.

Mr. Ogden went outside the Fort and watched anxiously until he saw them appear in the distance, accompanied by a large band of heavily armed Nez Perces. The Indian women carried the younger Spalding children in front of them on their horses, and it was a joyous sight to all to see them ride in.

Mr. and Mrs. Spalding went immediately to see their daughter Eliza, and found her greatly changed from the healthy, lively child they had left only one month ago.

Friday night, Catherine, Elizabeth, and Mary Smith, along with several others, were in Mrs. McBain's room when Mr. McBain came in and locked the doors and darkened the windows, telling them not, under any circumstances, to let the Indians see them, and to be very careful of what they said, as "the very walls have ears."

Every precaution was taken to prevent an attack. Mr. Ogden was afraid the Indians would try to get the survivors back to hold as hostages, if they heard the Americans were coming.

The next day the Indians came to the Fort to close the Treaty and receive their ransom. There were strict orders for the rescued to stay out of sight of the Indians.

Meanwhile, Edward tried three times to see Mary Smith, but she refused. McBain told her he thought her very hard-hearted. Edward was weeping as though his heart would break and Mary said, "What do I care for his tears?"

The Indians camped in the stockade of the Fort and kept up their war dance all night. But early the next morning they had all left.

Just at daybreak, January 2nd, the survivors were marched down to the boats and loaded into three large bateaus, each rowed by eight expert French Canadian oarsmen. When leaving the Fort, to protect Mr. Spalding, the men formed a square around him. Just as they were leaving, a band of Cayuse Indians came riding furiously, yelling their fierce war cry. The Nez Perces were already on their horses, ready to leave for their own country. When they saw the Cayuses coming, they formed a line between them and the boats and, waiting until the Cayuses got near, gave an unearthly war whoop! The Cayuses halted abruptly in astonishment, then turned and went back faster than they had come.

Mr. Ogden then ordered the oarsmen to row to the other side of the river as fast as they could. The Fort fired a cannon, partly as a salute to Mr. Ogden, and partly as a warning to the Indians. Mr. Ogden's boat took the lead and he signaled the oarsmen to row rapidly until they were well away from the Fort.

In Mr. Ogden's boat were Mr. Spalding and family, the Sager children, Lorinda Bewley, Mrs. Saunders and family, Little Mary Marsh, Mary Johnson, and Mr. J. H. Stanley, a young American artist, sent to paint pictures of the Indians. It was he who took upon himself the care of the little Sager children.

When they went ashore at night, Stanley would unbuckle his holsters and hand them to Catherine. He called her his "armor bearer." Then he would take little Henrietta in his arms and carry her to the encampment, wrap the children up, seat them near the fire and see that they had something to eat. Elizabeth said that she did not believe she would have lived through the trip down the river had it not been for his care.

Mr. Ogden, at all times, kept a sharp lookout for Indians. He was a large, portly man with an inexhaustible fund of good humor, and his jokes and stories did much to cheer the rescued. He laughed a lot about his large family as he called them and often would signal the boatmen to sing their French Canadian boat songs. Lorinda Bewley said afterwards, "No music in this world would ever sound so beautiful."

The boats now neared the rapids above Celilo, ancient Indian fishing grounds. An Indian village was here but the Indians were peaceable. They made portage here, the boats being unloaded and carried upside down on the heads of the oarsmen. The next day, about noon, they reached The Dalles, a Methodist Mission.

Within fifteen hours after the news of the massacre reached Oregon City, fifty volunteers were on their way to guard The Dalles, and this group was there when the boats arrived. Among the volunteers were many friends and relatives of the rescued. Little Mary Marsh was overjoyed to meet her brother, then seventeen years old, her only relative in Oregon. He told her that when he returned he would find her a good home. This promise he kept, finding Mary a home with Mrs. Asa Lovejoy.*

Mary Johnson also met her brother. Her father and mother were at Oregon City.

The rescued stopped at The Dalles but a short time, as Mr. Ogden insisted on making as rapid time as was possible. They camped that night a few miles below The Dalles and just at daybreak the next morning, the big boats headed down the broad and placid Columbia River, now famed in song and story.

Not a sound was heard save for the dipping of the oars. Down past the brown hills of Lyle, where now sleeps Frederick Homer Balch, beside his Genevieve . . . past Memaloose Island, the place of the dead, ancient burial ground of Indian

---

*Mr. Lovejoy was the one companion of Marcus Whitman on his famous Winter's ride to Washington, D. C., in 1842.

tribes. Next day they came to the Cascades, now famed through Indian legend, as the place where the Bridge of the Gods fell. Here they had to unload the boats and walk around the rapids about one mile, while the boats were lowered over the Cascades by ropes. They camped here that night and the next morning loaded the boats again and shot the rapids. It was while camped here that a messenger brought news of the death of Lorinda's father, Captain Bewley.

The boats now glided into smooth water again; the scenery changed. The hills became lofty mountains, covered with tall fir and pine, that seemed to meet the clouds that hovered over them. They passed numerous waterfalls rushing hundreds of feet down the mountain sides. Gazing upon this beautiful scene, the rescued almost forgot their sorrow for a time.

After passing Crown Point, the scene again began to change. Lofty mountains gave place to low hills and valleys, stately cottonwood trees lined the banks of the river. And smoke curled up from Indian wigwams.

The next day they neared Fort Vancouver and when they came in sight of the Fort, the boatmen began to sing with a zest that showed their joy at safely reaching home.

The rescued were very kindly received by Mr. Douglas and other members of the Fort. Mr. Spalding and family, Lorinda Bewley, and the Sager children were entertained by Mr. and Mrs. Douglas. Mrs. Douglas wished to keep Elizabeth and raise her with her children because she said, "Elizabeth speaks such good English."

Another woman at the Fort wished to take both Catherine and little Henrietta. Mr. Spalding objected to this, as the volunteer parents were Catholics, and he did not like them. Mr. Ogden also opposed the plan, saying he intended delivering all the rescued to the American Governor, and afterwards they could go where they wished.

While they were at the Fort, Mr. Stanley came every day to see the Sager children, and Elizabeth said he brought them material to make each of them a dress. On Monday afternoon, Peter Skeen Ogden started for Oregon City to deliver those he had rescued to Governor Abernathy.

During their entire journey down the Columbia, the survivors were seldom out of sight of stately Mt. Hood, which seemed to stand, a watchful sentinel looking down upon the little band with sorrowful mein. As they entered the Willamette, the mountain stood out sharp and clear, and seemed to smile and wave them onward!

They rowed across the wide Columbia, past Sauvies Island, ancient home of the Multnomah Indians, and into the beautiful Willamette. The island and surrounding waters were covered with stately white swans.

From the Cascades frozen gorges,
Leaping like a child at play,
Winding, widening through the Valley,
Bright Willamette glides away.
Onward ever,
Lovely river,
Softly calling to the sea;
Time that scars us,
Maims and mars us,
Leaves no track or trench on thee.

Spring's green witchery is weaving
Braid and border for thy side;
Grace forever haunts thy journey,
Beauty dimples on thy tide;
Through the purple gates of morning,
Now thy roseate riffles dance.
Golden then, when day, departing,
On thy waters trails his lance.
Waltzing, flashing,
Tinkling, splashing,
Limpid, volatile, and free —

Always hurried
To be buried
In the bitter, moon-mad sea.

SAM SIMPSON.

On Tuesday afternoon, January 10, they arrived at Portland, at that time a thriving young town boasting two white houses. Governor Abernathy and hundreds of settlers had gathered here to welcome Mr. Ogden and the survivors, lining the entire western side of the Willamette. On the Eastern side of the river were encamped 500 volunteers, on their way to capture the murderers of Dr. Marcus and Narcissa Whitman.

The volunteers formed a line along the shore and fired a salute. The salute frightened the little children, as they thought it was another massacre. The people gave three cheers which were heartily responded to from the boats. Some of the volunteers crossed to the West side where another salute was fired.

Colonel Gilliam, commander of the volunteers, put out in a small boat and boarded Mr. Ogden's boat. He asked Mr. Ogden to point out the Sager children to him. He had crossed the plains with them, and knew their parents well. When he landed, he came back to the children and talked to them kindly.

Captain Shaw, former guardian of the children, also came forward and greeted them. He and his three sons were with the Volunteers, and many others they knew came to greet them. Elizabeth said afterwards that it then seemed there were some left in their sad world that cared for them.

Governor Abernathy invited Mr. Spalding and family, along with the Sager children, to his home at Green Point, a short distance from Oregon City on the Willamette River. They stayed with the Abernathys until suitable homes were found for them. Although the children were separated for the first time, they found friendly homes, and lived long, useful lives and left many proud descendants.

Lorinda Bewley was met by William Chapman, to whom she was engaged, and taken to her mother. Lorinda was overjoyed to see her family again, and as soon as she recovered her health, she taught school. When young Chapman returned from the war, the California gold rush was on. He went to the mines and upon his return he and Lorinda were married, and lived on his donation land claim in the beautiful Tualatin Valley. Many of their descendants still live around Sheridan and Portland, Oregon.

When the Volunteers reached the Umatilla, they sent out word to all the Indian tribes that they did not come to make war, but to punish those who had taken part in the massacre.

The Volunteers were met by a large band of Indians led by Chief Five Crows and Chief Grey Eagle who rode in front of the main band. Grey Eagle dared the Americans to shoot and Tom McKay shot him through the heart. Charley McKay shot Five Crows off his horse, severely wounding him.

Several years later Five Crows came down into the Willamette Valley to sell horses, went to see Charlie McKay, and told him he bore him no hard feelings, that he got what he deserved.

The Indians rushed forward and carried Five Crows to the lodge of his half-brother, old Chief Joseph of the Nez Perces. The Indians then retreated back into the mountains and after a bit of skirmishing, the fighting came to an end.

When Spring came the snow in the mountains melted and the Cayuse Indians could now go almost anywhere to avoid capture. The soldiers built a fort in the Cayuse country and drove the Indians from their homes. They were told that their lands would be occupied until they gave up the murderers. The heart of the Cayuse was not in this war with his white brothers, but some Indian loyalty caused them to persist in protecting the murderers.

Finally old Chief Joseph,* carrying a white flag, came to meet the soldiers with a large band of Nez Perces and Cayuses.

"I have heard the words of your Chief," he said. "I do not want war. I speak for all the Cayuses present and for my people. I do not want my children to engage in this war, although my brother Five Crows is wounded. You speak of the murderers. I shall not meddle with them. I bow my head. This much I speak."

When the news of the massacre reached Oregon City, then the seat of government in Oregon, Joe Meek, a famous mountain man, volunteered to carry the news to Washington. He also carried with him a petition from the settlers asking that the Laws of the United States Government be extended over the Oregon Territory. Accompanied by one companion, Squire Ebberts, he went with the troops as far as Waiilatpu where he helped bury the bodies that had been dug up by the wolves. Among these was little Helen Mar Meek, his half breed daughter who had died from the measles. After burying the dead, he rode on to Washington where the news he brought aroused the United States government to action, and they extended their protection over the Oregon Territory. The fighting Joe Lane was appointed the first territorial Governor, and Joe Meek as United States Marshal. They returned to Oregon the next Fall, and the new Governor Lane at once took measures to capture the murderers.

The Cayuse tribe could not return to their homes, and they suffered many hardships. A little over two years after the massacre they decided to give up the murderers to officers of the government. Only five were left as some had died and others had been killed.

---

*Old Chief Joseph was the father of the famous Chief Joseph, of the Nez Perce War with the Americans in the 70's.

Members of the Cayuse and Nez Perces tribe delivered were Chief Teloukaike, Tamayhas, Clackamus, Left-Hand, and Wet Wolf, five of the murderers, who were delivered to Governor Lane at the Cascades. They were promptly taken to Oregon City and jailed. Catherine Sager was taken to the jail to identify the Indians, and she called each one by name at once. Teloukaike tried to talk to her, but she had forgotten their language and could not understand him. Some of them shed tears.*

The five murderers offered many horses and blankets for lawyers to defend them. They were tried by a jury, found guilty, and all five were hung June 3, 1850. Lorinda Chapman, Elizabeth and Catherine, and other survivors appeared as witnesses against the Indians.

Five Crows recovered from his wounds and came back to his home on the Umatilla, a sad and broken-hearted man. He took no part in Indian affairs, but lived alone. An old Indian woman told this writer, "Five Crows sits in his lodge and cries — cries about his white wife."

From the writings of Perrin Whitman, nephew of Dr. Whitman, Joe Lewis took all the money from the belongings of the murdered captives. He then wished to leave as he feared the Indians might suspect him of treachery and disloyalty, and that his life might be in danger. After the prisoners were delivered to Fort Walla Walla, he proposed to the Indians that four of those that had taken part in the massacre accompany him to the land of the Mormons. These people, he told them, would come back with him and help kill the Americans, and this seemed quite plausible to the Indians. Edward, Clark, Frank and other Indians accompanied Joe Lewis, and they journeyed up the Snake River,

---

*Some of the later writers are saying these Indians were not the guilty ones, but what better evidence than the testimony of those who were present at the Massacre and knew the Indians well.

crossed the Blue Mountains into the Grand Ronde Valley. At this point, one Indian was sent back by Lewis, on the pretext that the Mormons might be alarmed and suspect some treachery if so many of them went. Near what is now Pocatello, Idaho, Joe Lewis killed the three remaining Indians, and took their horses, blankets and money.

Angus McDonald, a Hudson's Bay man at Fort Hall, while en route to Fort Walla Walla, came upon these Indians, and recognized them as Teloukaike's sons, Edward and Clark, and an influential Indian named Frank. They were lying in a row with their rifles beside them, and had evidently been killed in their sleep.

After the murderers were delivered to Governor Lane, the Cayuse tribe returned to their homes. Seven years later, the white people began to settle North of the Columbia, the Hudson's Bay Company having given up their forts and left the territory. The American government now bought the land from the Indians, and the Indians were put on Reservations.

Joel Palmer, Indian Agent, was with the Americans who moved the Indians. Of the affair, he said, "Sunday morning, Chief Stickus rang his bell and 45 Cayuses met with him in worship. At the station of Mr. Spalding, 1,000 Nez Perces met with Chief Timothy for worship. Mr. Spalding was prevented for 23 years from going to his beloved Nez Perces. At last he was returned to them, and was received with open arms.

Mr. Spalding held a great revival and baptized hundreds of Indians. Later he died, and he and his wife are buried at Lapwai and to this day their graves are cared for by the Nez Perces.

Thus ends one of the saddest tragedies in Western history.

APPENDICES

NEW LIGHT THROWN ON WHITMAN DEATH

Massacre of Missionary Recalled by Letter.—Survivor Gives Story.—Elizabeth M. Sager, at Age of 18, *Tells of Pitiful Journey That Ends in Sudden Tragedy.*

A new version of the Whitman massacre has been made available to Pacific Northwest historians through the courtesy of Marion Sager and Mrs. Ruth Wilson, of Seymour, Iowa.

The account is provided through a letter written at Salem, Oregon, January 17, 1855, by Elizabeth M. Sager, to her uncle, Frederick Sager. Elizabeth Sager wrote the letter at the age of 18. She had been a survivor of the Whitman massacre eight years before.

Mrs. Ruth Wilson, Seymour, Iowa, sent a copy of the letter to *The Oregonian*, with this explanation:

Sager Family Prominent

"The Sager family were prominent pioneers of Wayne County, Iowa.

"Matilda Sager (a maternal grandmother of Ben F. Dorris, Portland), and her sisters were among the few survivors of the Whitman massacre in 1847.

"Marion Sager, of Seymour, Iowa, a first cousin of Matilda Sager and her sisters, has in his possession a letter descriptive of the Whitman massacre which he kindly gave permission to copy for publication. Mr. Sager is the last of his generation."

The letter written by Elizabeth Sager follows:

Salem, Or., January 17, 1855.—Dear Uncle: There is something so novel in writing to you, my unknown friend, that I hardly know how to commence. I was greatly surprised in getting a letter from my relatives after so great a lapse of time. Brother John used to take me on his knee and tell me over the names of my uncles and I distinctly remember Uncle Frederick's name, and this is all I know of my friends. And as I have now heard of you I will give you a short history of our lives. We started on our road to Oregon in the year 1844. If I mistake not it was in the month of April. Mother was not well when we started. She said she would not live to get through. Father gave her choice of come to Oregon or go back to Indiana, and she said she would rather come to Oregon. In May after we started she had a little baby. She was sick from that time on till she died. When we got to Fort Laramie we met with a sad misfortune; sister Catherine fell out of the wagon and shivered her leg all to pieces. She went to get out of the wagon and her dress caught on the ax-handle and she fell and the fore wheels ran right over her leg and back; fortunately it did not injure her back any. It went very hard with mother. Father set the leg himself. He would not trust the care to any of the doctors. It healed without ever making her lame. Father was taken sick I think on Platte River; he caused his sickness by chasing some buffalo on a very hot day. Just as we crossed Green River he died.

Sister Catherine was sick at the time with her leg. A few days before he died he laid his hand on her head and said, "Poor child, what will become of you when your father dies?" and those were the last words he ever spoke to her. Mother lived just 21 days after father died. She left us in care of an old Dutch doctor, and told him to take us to the first mission. He promised her faithfully, with the tears running down his cheeks, that he would take care of us as if we were his own children. He was very kind to us and kept his promise. We arrived at Dr. Whitman's station on the 17th day of October, 1844, and here the good doctor left us. There was seven children of us all. First was John, 14; Francis, 12; Catherine, 9; Elizabeth, 7; Matilda, 5; Louise, 3, and Henrietta, who was the little babe born on the road, 5 months. This was quite a large and helpless family for one man to take. He adopted us all, and treated us as if we were his own children. We always called them father and mother. They had no children of their own. The boys were going to come on down with the emigration and live in the valley until they were old enough to hold a claim; then they were going to send for us girls and take care of us themselves, but Dr. Whitman persuaded them to give up the idea and live with him. He said he would not have the girls unless he could have the boys, too. We lived there three years very happily, when on the fateful 29th of November, 1847, we were doomed to witness what I pray I may never behold again, the murder of my beloved brothers and adopted father and mother and 11 emigrants. It makes my blood run cold to think of it. We were all sick with the measles at the time. Louisa and Henrietta were not expected to live from one hour to another.

Time of Massacre Recalled

The massacre commenced at 1 o'clock in the day Monday. I had just gone from the kitchen into the dining room when all at once I heard a great firing in the room I had just left. Mrs. Whitman threw up her hands and exclaimed, "The Indians are killing us." An Indian had called the doctor out in the kitchen just a little before, under a pretense of wanting medicine, and the firing was at him. Brother John was in there at the time, winding a ball of twine. When I saw him he was a lifeless corpse. When the firing ceased Mrs. Whitman stepped into the kitchen and dragged father into the dining room and asked him if she could do anything for him. He whispered, "No," and it was the last word he spoke. As she was passing into the parlor to get some ashes to put on his mangled head to stop the blood, she stepped to the window to see what was going on, an Indian raised his gun and a ball went right through her right side. I was standing by her at the time. It seemed to me almost a miracle that it did not go right through my head. Mother dropped where she was standing and did not think of herself, for her prayer was, "Oh, my dear children, what will become of you." How I pitied her; I could not cry, I could not move. Presently I was aroused by the crashing of windows and mother exclaimed, "Take them all upstairs." Mr. Rogers, although he was wounded very badly, motioned for all of us to run upstairs while he gathered up the sick children to bring them up, and when he got them up he went back for mother. An Indian came and called for them to come downstairs, that they were going to set the house on fire. But they did not go down, as the Indian came upstairs. He told mother that he was her friend and not to fear anything, to come down immediately for they were going to burn the house, so they went, myself and several of the women with them.

When we got down mother was laid on a settee to be taken over to the other house, where the emigrants stayed. Mr. Rogers and a half breed by the name of Joe Lewis each took one end of the settee. The Indians came in and shook their blankets, saying, "We have no guns, you need not be afraid." We stepped into the kitchen and saw the lifeless body of brother John lying on his face in the doorway. We had to step over him as we passed out. When we got on the front steps I looked around and saw a row of Indians along the wall ready to fire as soon as their victims should appear; I turned around and ran upstairs as fast as I could. I slipped in the blood as I went; there was blood all over the wall by brother John. The Indians told us he fought desperately for his life. We children stayed upstairs till the next day. The Indian that got mother and Mr. Rogers to go down told us that Francis had run away; that they did not kill him. Just as we were passing through the room, there lay Francis, dead. Sister Kate was afraid to go on; she said the Indians were going to kill us as they did mother last night. I did not feel afraid somehow; I felt that they would not touch us. I was frightened more when the Catholic priest came, as he said, to see that they were buried decently. I felt more afraid of him than of the Indians. The bodies lay out in the yard three days before they were buried. I went over with Lorinda and took a last look at my brothers. Five days after Dr. Whitman was killed Louisa died. I went to see her buried, though the women tried hard to keep me from going. We were there prisoners four weeks when Mr. Ogden, a Hudson's Bay man, came and bought us from them. I expect you will think this not a very good description of the massacre, but when I write again I will give you all the particulars. Matilda knows more about it than I do.

Aftermath Proves Hard

I will write to you her evidence next time I write to you. When I came down into the valley I went to live with a man by the name of Robb. I lived with him two years, when he wanted to take his family to California. I did not want to go, so I went to live with a man by the name of Wilson. I lived there a year, but they were so unkind to me I would not stay any longer. So I went to live with Mr. Parish. His wife made a great fuss one day because I wanted to go and see my sister Matilda. Sister Catherine was going and wanted me to go with her. We had not seen her but once in four years, and you may be sure that I wanted to see her very much. Sister Catherine had just been married a few months to a man by the name of Clark Pringle. When we came back from the plains Mrs. Parish told me that I could not live with her any more, so brother Clark took me to live with them. I have lived with them three years now. I support myself by teaching school, that is, I get my own clothes. Sister Catherine has one little girl. Her name is Kate Virginia. Henrietta lives with Clark, too. Matilda lives with Mr. Giger at the Tualatin plains, 50 miles from us. I have not seen her but three times since we came from Dr. Whitman's. She wrote me that she would be married sometime in February to a Mr. Hazlett, who is 30, while she is only 15. I expect you will think this is a funny match, but is nothing in Oregon. I have a great many questions to ask you and some of them I expect you will think very silly, but I have such a curiosity to know everything. When you write to me I want you to answer all of them if you can. I want to know if you are a married man and, if so, who you married; if you have any children and what their names are, how many brothers my father had and their wives' names and what my grandmother's name was before she was married, also what grandfathers' two other wives' names were. I want to know what my father's age would have been had he lived, also mother's age. What state were they born in and what day and month. If you have it, please send me a lock of father's and mother's hair also of your own and dear grandfather's. Sister Catherine wrote you a letter on the 24th of December. She gave you more particulars than I can, as she was older and remembers more than I do. She sent you a lock of all our hair. Could you send us grandfather's daguerrotype? We would prize it highly, as it was grandfather himself. I always thought he was dead, and was very much surprised when you wrote to us that he was alive yet. I will send you three pieces of my hair. Please give one lock to grandfather and tell him to keep it to remember his little granddaughter; give one of the other locks to your oldest daughter if you have any, if not keep it yourself. Give the other lock to some of my cousins if I have any. Write to me as soon as you get this letter, if you please, and give me all the particulars.

Your affectionate niece,

ELIZABETH M. SAGER.

LETTER FROM CATHERINE SAGER PRINGLE

Following is a letter written by Catherine Sager Pringle, dated at Salem, Oregon, December 21, 1854, a principal in the foregoing story:

Catherine Sager was the eldest daughter of Henry and Naomi Sager, who started across the plains to Oregon in 1844. Both parents died before reaching the end of their journey and the seven orphan children found refuge at the Whitman mission and remained there until the massacre in 1847. The two boys, John and Francis, were killed in the massacre and one girl died a few days later. Catherine and her three sisters were brought to Oregon City with the other survivors. They could no longer be together, but were placed with different families. Catherine found a home with the Reverend William Roberts. A son of Mr. Roberts wrote to his grandparents in New Jersey, mentioning by name the orphan girl who had become a member of his household. His letter was printed in the Methodist paper, the *Christian Advocate.* Frederick Sager saw it, and remembering that his brother Henry had a daugh-er Catherine, addressed a letter to "Catherine Sager, Somewhere in Oregon," and sent it across the plains by an immigrant. It was finally posted at Salem and there she received it. The letter below is Catherine's answer, giving her uncle news of herself and sisters and a vivid account of the Whitman massacre as she remembered it.

The original letter, of which this is a copy, is owned by Charles F. Keezer, Ericson, Nebraska, whose mother was a first cousin of Catherine Sager Pringle.

Salem, Dec. 21, 1854

Dear Uncle:

We received your letter yesterday. You can hardly realize with what pleasure we have made inquiry of everyone we saw from Ohio. You wished in the first place to know how many of us remain. There are four of us, Catherine, Elizabeth, Matilda Jane and Henrietta Naomi. In the second place you asked where we were. I am married and am living on a farm four miles from Salem. I was married to Clark Spencer

Pringle on the 25th of October, 1851. We own a full section of land, that is 640 acres. Elizabeth and Henrietta have been living with us ever since we were married. Matilda lives with a family about 30 miles from here by the name of Geiger. She has lived in his family seven years. She is like a daughter to them. She will be married in the course of a few months to Lewis Hazlett. Elizabeth is teaching school. She has taught off and on for the last three years. I do not know whether she will marry soon or not. She is engaged but will not marry she says till she has made something. I will be 20 years old on the 17th of next April. E will be 18 the 16th of July. M will be 16 the 6th of October. H will be 11 the 22nd of May. She was a baby 5 months old when mother died in the Spring of 44. We started for Oregon in good heart and spirits about July 1 I think it was. I fell out of the wagon, the wheels passing over me broke one leg very badly. Father would not allow a doctor to be called but set and tended it himself. I have got over it now so I hardly limp at all to the suprise of all that knew me then. A lady who was present at the time told me a few days ago that she never expected to see me live. In a few days after this accident father took what they called the yellow fever, a species of the camp fever, of which he died. He put his family in care of the captain of the company and requested him to leave them at Dr. Whitmans. I was too young then to notice dates so I cannot tell you when he died, but I think it was in August. Mother's health to here was very feeble at the time of his death and the care of the family of seven children, one a baby and me helpless and as much trouble as an infant, besides perplexities of travelling, soon broke her down. She became delirious before she took to her bed and at times was perfectly insane. The way she called and moaned and called her Henry during these spells was heart rending and I shall never forget it but, poor woman, she did not have long to mourn for in 26 days she followed her beloved husband. A few days before she died she was conscious and bid us all adieu; told us that we must be good children; she then called the driver of our team and told him to take her children over to Dr. Whitmans and he did so. She then became unconscious and remained so till she died. She died so easy no one knew for hours that she was dead but supposed her to be sleeping. She was buried without a coffin on the banks of Willow Creek and many tears were shed by the kind hearted company for the poor little orphans that stood around her grave. We were all taken care of by the company. There was not one but that would share their bread with us. We arrived at Dr. Whitmans the 17th of October. They could not find it in their hearts to refuse the dying request of our parents nor give a headless ear to our urgent request not to be parted. They took the whole seven. They had no children of their own but they had orphans enough to make eleven. We called them father and mother and so they were to us while they lived. We were all fed, well clothed, and sent to school every winter. They took every means to make us happy. They employed a teacher in the family every winter. We lived there about three years and a half, that is till 47, when by a mysterious stroke of providence we were again thrown upon the wide world without home and deprived of two dearly beloved brothers and a much petted sister Hannah Loisa.

The emigration of 47 brought the measles among the Indians and great numbers of them died. I have known five to be buried in one day. The Catholic Priest had come among them; also Dr. Whitman had taken into his family a half breed that had come in with the emigration. This person, the priest and the measles all combined brought about the massacre. Poor Doctor rode about all day tending the sick natives and all night he was up with his family and other white folks that had stopped at his station to winter. Everyone of his family was down at once excepting the half breed I have told you of whose name was Joe Lewis, and his wife. Joe Lewis told the Indians that the Dr. was poisoning them. On Saturday night before the massacre Dr. and Mr. Spalding, his colleague, started for the Umatilla River about 25 miles from home to see some sick Indians and were gone all the next day. At about 10 o'clock Sunday night Dr. came back. My Brothers were sitting up with us they having got well. Mrs. Whitman had been up all the night before with Henrietta who was supposed to be dying. I remember just how my dear brother looked as, with their shoes off for fear of making a noise, they moved around waiting on us for it was the last time I ever saw them alive. As soon as the Dr. came they went to bed. He looked at each child and when he came to Helen, a little girl living with him, he called Mrs. Whitman and told her that Helen was dying. He sat down and watched her until she finally got better. He told Mrs. W. that an Indian named Sticus had told him that that evening the Indians were talking of killing him! that Joe Lewis was putting them up to it. He spent a sleepless night for he was in trouble. The next day, which was the fatal 29th of November, he was talking and said if things did not look brighter by April he was going to leave, but, said he, "If I am to die by the hands of Catholics my death will do more good than my life."

After giving some directions in reference to the children, three of whom were past hope, the little girl I spoke of above and my two youngest sisters, he went to bury an Indian. When he came back he said the Indians were gathering about but he supposed it was because they were killing a beef that day and they always came on such days to get what was thrown away. He said that none of them were at the funeral. He went upstairs to see a young lady who was sick. He found her crying bitterly but she could not tell why. He came down and stood at the window a few moments as in deep thought and then said "poor L." is in trouble and cannot tell why. I will get her some medicine and you had better go and talk to her awhile." He went to the medicine case to get some. While Mrs. W. went into the pantry to get some milk the Indians crowded around demanding some. She told them to wait till she gave some to her children. She then came into the sitting room where we were and locked the door after her as the Indians were not allowed in that room. They still kept asking for the milk and Mrs. W. started to get some for them. Just as she got to the door they asked for the Dr. She said "Dr. you are wanted." He went out and she fastened the door after him. Presently we heard a very loud talk in the kitchen but paid no attention to it till we heard a gun go off and immediately followed by another one. We could not tell what it was but started to run. Mrs. W. called us back and started for the kitchen exclaiming "Oh they have killed my husband." By this time the shooting had become general. Mrs. W. brought a pillow and put it under his head. He was not dead. She asked him if he knew her. He said "yes." She asked him if she could do anything to stop the bleeding. He said no. "Can you speak to me?" He said "no."

Mr. Rodgers, a young man living with us, now came in with his arm broken and Mrs. W. was standing at the window looking out at the slaughter without when a ball hit her in the shoulder. She screamed and fell to the floor but her wound did not trouble her. It was her children. "Oh what will become of my little ones! Lord, save these little ones," came in heart rending tones from her lips time and again. I was standing looking over her shoulder a minute before she was shot but seeing the Indians trying to kill the school teacher I could not stand it and went upstairs. Mr. Rodgers carrying the sick children and then helping Mrs. W. to get up. The Indians now broke into the house. After looking all over they broke in the stairway door. We placed a broken gun over the bannister as if to shoot. They were frightened and retired. For the space of an hour all was still as death except the low voice of Mr. R. engeged in prayer for the safety of all.

We now heard footsteps approaching as one in great haste. They stopped at the door and a voice called Mr. Rodgers. He did not answer. The Indians kept calling and he finally answered and asked what he wanted. The Indian told him that he had nothing to do with the massacre and wanted Mr. R. to come down which he refused to do, desiring him to come up there but the Indians said that he would not; that we had white folks up there that would kill him. After much parley Mr. R. finally went to the bottom of the stairs and talked with and finally got him upstairs. He shook hands with us all; was very sorry for what had happened, especially Mrs. W. being shot. He then told us he wanted us to leave the house as the Indians were going to burn it down. He appeared so kind we begun to get ready to go, Mrs. W. saying "God has raised us up a friend." He told us children to wait until he came back.

They all went down leaving us and a wounded man but they hardly got outside the door into the yard when the treacherous mortal friends fired on them, killing Mr. R., Mrs. W. and brother Francis. He had with the other children who had got well enough been in school when the massacre commenced. They all climbed into the loft. When the Indians took the other children down he stayed up there and had he only remained until night he might have escaped but his anxiety respecting his sister would not allow him to stay. He came down and the first thing he saw was his brother lying on the floor shot and his throat cut and his tippet stuffed into the wound. Francis pulled the tippet out. John tried to speak but died in the attempt. Francis burst into tears and taking sister Matilda by the hand said "I will soon follow my brother." He was shot soon after by Joe Lewis. But why dwell on these awful scenes or try to describe the night we spent in that chamber or our feeling when, next morning, surrounded by murderers we looked at the mangled corpses of our beloved second parents and our brothers.

I have given you a short account of this horrible massacre but to give you a definite idea of it is impossible. They were buried the following Wednesday in one large grave but it was so shallow the wolves dug them up before we left and their bones are scattered. About five days after this Louisa died. We lived prisoners a month when we were ransomed by Mr. Ogden of the Hudson's Bay Company. He died lately. It was with joy mingled with tears that we bid farewell to the home that had been so pleasant and the place of so much calamity. We arrived at Oregon City in January and were loudly saluted by the troops on their way to make war with the Indians. The war continued some time and was finally concluded by their giving five of the chief murderers who were hung in Oregon City. The poor fellows shed tears when they found they had to swing but it did no good. They wanted to be shot but hanging was the law.

We all found homes right off but had to be parted. I lived with Rev. W. Roberts and was the girl spoken of in the *Advocate* you spoke of. I lived with them till I was married and they did well by me. Matilda had lived in the same place all the time. E and H have changed places several times so after all here I am settled down in sober married life and a girl with blue eyes calls me by the name of ma.

We hear by the emigrants that came the year after that the Indians had robbed fathers' grave, leaving his bones to bleach on the prairie.

Perhaps you would like to know something of this country. We have had up to this time very little rain, the nights being cold, the sun shining warm and pleasant during the day. Crops are generally good. Times are rather dull there being no cash in the country. Wheat is six bits a bushel in cash and a dollar in trade. Potatoes are 25 to 50 cents per bushel. Wages are from one to two dollars per day. There is too much merchandise in the country and no public improvements. We would like very much to have grandpas dageurreotype if you would send it to us and as many more as you are able to send us. We want to know how our kin folks look. I want you to write and tell us how many uncles and aunts we have and their names. Have you any children? What are our cousins names and how many of them? What is grandpas name and what was grandmas name? How old was father when he died and where was he born? Also what was mother's age.

I did not tell you the name of our daughter. We call her Kate Virginia. I have written you a long letter but it was necessary to let you know our history. Remember us to all the relations and tell them to write. Direct your letters to Salem, Marion Co., O. T.

CATHERINE SAGER PRINGLE.

To Frederic Sager